On the Journey to Wholeness

On the Journey to Wholeness

Cabbage Grows from the Inside Out

Eugene Friesen and Carroll Rinehart

Press, LLC

Good Oak Press, LLC
P.O. Box 12195
Tucson, Arizona 85732

Cover Design: Good Oak Press, LLC
Typesetting: Good Oak Press, LLC

ISBN: 978-0-9839384-1-5

CONTENTS

ACKNOWLEDGEMENTS

This book has been in the making for more than twenty years. We were absorbed in our professional lives and would put the book aside for months at a time. Even though months passed, we were invariably drawn back to the concepts central to this book, along with our professional and personal experiences. We are most indebted to the persons who have been our teachers. In most cases, they were totally unaware of the role they were playing. We have attempted to share their stories which, in so many ways, have shaped our professional growth and have added immeasurably to this book.

Over time, we have invited colleagues to read what we had written. We received enough affirmation and reinforcement to continue. The person to which we, the authors, are most indebted is Vaughn Huff, Ph.D., a retired psychology professor at the University of Arizona. He spent countless hours editing our writing, raising hard questions, offering alternative ways of presenting what we were trying to say when our writing seemed unclear and, most of all, encouraging us to continue. Without his skillful and thoughtful guidance, it is doubtful we would have completed this work.

Leland Scott, Ph.D., an ordained United Methodist minister and a retired college counselor and instructor, helped with proof reading as well as making editorial suggestions on this manuscript. The authors are deeply appreciative of his contributions.

In discussing the theme of this book with the late Reverend Dewane Zimmerman, then the Senior Minister at the First United Methodist Church in Phoenix, he made the suggestion that grace precedes the processes of confession, repentance, forgiveness, and reconciliation. His observation led to our including a chapter on the dynamics of grace. Dr. Bill Hillman, Professor of Counseling & Guidance at the University of Arizona, now retired, provided affirmation for the practical use of this book through his use of the unpublished manuscript in his work with clients.

The concepts of Psychosynthesis, originated by the Italian psychiatrist Roberto Assagioli, have been central to our writing. Psychosynthesis was introduced to us while Eugene was participating in a D Min program through the Jesuit School of Theology, Berkeley, California; Carroll was one of a dozen individuals active as a support group in this program. While Assagioli, a contemporary of both Freud and Jung, never achieved the notoriety that these psychoanalytic giants did, he nevertheless had a powerful, if more subtle, influence on what has been referred as the third force in the psychological world.

The impact of Dr Robert Keck's writing, *Sacred Eyes* (1992) and *Sacred Quest: The Evolution and Future of the Human Soul* (2000), has significantly impacted our thoughts and our writing. For us, he has provided the theoretical framework for the growth of the holistic health movement. His developmental look at the human story, as well as at the evolving universe, is nothing short of revolutionary. We are deeply in his debt.

Eugene Friesen and Carroll Rinehart *

* Note: A small (#) in the text will indicate a source note to be found on pages 166 – 167.

PREFACE

What does it mean to be whole? Where does the inner longing for wholeness, that persistently haunts us in the quieter moments at all stages of life, come from? How can this inner hunger and thirst be satisfied? What are the blocks to wholeness? It was through our attempt to give meaning to many experiences of life, and in the quest for a fuller, richer existence, that we began asking such questions and studying what others questing for meaning had said. Readings, workshops, dialogues with friends all gave greater focus and guidance to our search. Participation in the Growth Group models of the 60s and 70s, small groups of individuals gathered to assist each other in psychological and spiritual development, provided us with a rich background in the concepts and methods of Transactional Analysis, Gestalt psychology. These, and other models, offered us many options for consideration and experimentation.

However, it was the work of Roberto Assagioli and his Psychosynthesis model which had the most significant impact on our thinking. Other influences on our orientation include the work of Milton Erickson, Donald Tubesing and Virginia Satir. More recently, as indicated in our Acknowledgements, we have been influenced by the work of Robert Keck.

Our synthesis of these various influences led us to conclude that wholeness involves one's psycho-emotional, transpersonal-spiritual, bio-physical, social-cultural and creative-intellectual aspects, all of which are dynamically interdependent. While an individual may consciously experience personal dysfunction in one of these areas, to assure that wholeness is achieved all aspects need to be explored.

Moreover, from his clinical work with clients, Dr. Friesen has observed that a predictable sequence of events occurs in the healing process. While these events in a secular sense are referred to in differing terms, they parallel the following theological sequence: confession, repentance, forgiveness and reconciliation. Dr. Friesen has also noted that before any of these occur, something equivalent to a state of grace must be present.

In this book, we have primarily used a story-telling style, that draws heavily on our own professional and personal experiences, to articulate what we see as the essence of the healing process. While we have been influenced by a psychological orientation that can be described as transpersonal and holistic, we have primarily confined our theoretical discussions to the Overview chapter, although the implications of this orientation can be seen throughout the book.

The organization of chapters that follow the Overview deal sequentially with what we see as developmental steps to healing. Each of these steps is explored through the various aspects of wholeness, using a variety of psychological and theological viewpoints. The content of the chapters provide a basis for understanding the relationships within and between the phases in the sequence

Proposed activities throughout the chapters afford readers opportunities to understand the information, then to experientially internalize the process and make it a part of their lives. Wherever the following notation occurs in the text (+++), the reader is urged to stop and reflect on some bit of information. For example, at this point take time to reflect on how you might expect this book to be helpful to you. The ability to process information is dependent upon a person's ability to find congruence in what is being read with that which is already internalized. Reflect for a moment about some of the things you have already experienced and know regarding your own journey to wholeness. (+++) Now make a list of some of the questions you have about your life which you hope may be answered in this book. (+++)

We invite you to share in these thoughts, feelings and insights. We hope that, in the chapters to follow, questions of significance will surface. These pages will have fully served their purpose when your questions reach beyond the thoughts we have posed. In our experience, the processes of change are better reflected by the question mark (?) than by the period (.) or exclamation point (!). We encourage you to question and to derive your own personally relevant understandings and practices leading to wholeness. Growth and change are inside jobs.

Chapter 1
OVERVIEW
GETTING STARTED

I bring a special gift to you.
And be it partial, whole
Depends in part on how you read
What goes within my soul.
My gift to you is made of words
Combined letters of the alphabet
I often use them carelessly,
Without much thought, and yet
Words are a very private thing.
My words are a part of me.
Words are a window to my soul
Through which I let you see.
[Carroll Rinehart]

MOST OF US HAVE EXPERIENCED deep-seated feelings of inadequacy accompanied by surges of panic or fear. In the midst of such waves of anxiety we have longed for a sense of wholeness.

Eugene:

In my younger years, I vividly remember trekking long, arduous miles through unexplored jungles in Surinam. The lines of an old Gospel hymn were surging unspoken in my being. 'Lord Jesus, I long to be perfectly whole…' In quiet moments since then, this longing for wholeness has emerged when I have allowed my frantic pace, undoubtedly a cover for my feeling of incompleteness, to slacken—moments when I have allowed myself access to my 'inward' parts.

In the pages that follow we will explore a variety of tools which focus on enhancing life qualities. More importantly, we will give you opportunities to experience that which contributes to more abundant life and energy.

A Pessimistic View

Sigmund Freud, whose pioneering safari into the unexplored terrain of unconscious motivation, has radically affected perceptions of human behavior. He tended to see persons as being controlled and driven by "baser instincts" whose origins were largely hidden to them. His pessimistic bent gave some affirmation to earlier theological postulates asserting that humans were essentially depraved. At best, these "baser instincts" could be sublimated or re-directed. Conscious awareness emerged as conceptual dikes erected to hold back the "dark waters" of the unconscious.

From Pessimism To Potential

Roberto Assagioli, the father of Psychosynthesis, was a contemporary of Freud as well as of Karl Jung. Much of Assagioli's work, drawing upon Jung's concepts of the levels of the conscious and unconscious, seems directed toward bringing the natural energies of the universe to play in our lives. While it is not our intention to fully articulate or be restricted to Assagioli's system of thought, we will lean heavily on some of his theoretical formulations. Without ignoring Freud's insights regarding the "twistedness" of unconscious forces, we will examine the creative potential of these natural energies and suggest strategies for redirecting them.

Psychosynthesis in a Nutshell

Psychosynthesis has focused on the use of meditation techniques as a way to dialogue with the unconscious. Somewhat comparable to the techniques of free association used in psychoanalysis, the imagery which flows becomes a way of visualizing the invisible, "enfleshing" that which is spirit. This visualization extends to what can be called our lower and higher selves. Sub-personalities (lower selves) are defined by James Vargiu, an interpreter of Assagioli, as a "synthesis of habit patterns, traits, complexes and other psychological elements."(1) Our sub-personalities were acquired initially to help us meet our needs.

Levels Of Unconsciousness

Assagioli identifies three levels of the unconscious: the lower unconscious, the middle unconscious, the higher unconscious. Another of his interpreters, Piero Ferrucci, suggests that the three horizontal divisions of the oval pictured below, to the right, represent our past, present and future. The lower unconscious primarily "represents our personal psychological past in the form of repressed compulsive and long forgotten memories."(2) He adds that this abstraction may represent stored repressed energy which can impact our actions and rob us of our freedom. This description bears a great deal of similarity to Freud's conceptualization.

The middle unconscious is that area poised between the lower unconscious and the higher unconscious. Assagioli states that it is "in this region our various experiences are assimilated, our ordinary mental and imaginative activities are elaborated and developed in a sort of psychological gestation before their birth into the light of consciousness. (3)

Carroll:

Often in the composing process, I have been aware of an emerging idea before it is fully formed. It is like it's there just below the surface of awareness but I'm not yet fully attuned to its presence.

The Personal Self, which is synonymous with the "I," is located within this "middle consciousness" and can deliberately be brought into our field of awareness. This awareness may come as a result of meditation and/or from inspiration. According to this schematic, the

"I" or the Personal Self is located inside the field of consciousness but is an outpost of the Transpersonal Self sometimes referred to as Universal Energy. The "I" becomes not only the conduit of this energy, but also the legitimate orchestrator of behavior.

Ferrucci states that the Transpersonal Self "... while retaining a sense of individuality, lives at the level of universality, in a realm where personal plans and concerns are overshadowed by a wider vision of the whole." He adds that the "... personal and transpersonal self are in fact the same reality experienced at different levels: our true essence beyond all masks and conditionings."(4)

The higher unconscious, sometimes called the super conscious, is that area from which we "receive our higher intuitions and inspirations—artistic, philosophical or scientific, ethical imperatives and the urge to humanitarian and heroic action. It is the source of the higher feelings such as altruistic love, of genius and of the states of contemplation, illumination and ecstasy."(5)

Assagioli acknowledges that we can repress some of our earlier conflicts in our lower unconscious. However, he points out that we also often repress the sublime and the holy within us. The distinction between the "lower" and "higher" unconscious is developmental, not moralistic. The lower unconscious represents the most primitive part of us. It is not bad, it is just earlier.

Sub-personalities

Ferrucci describes sub-personalities as "...psychological satellites, coexisting as a multitude of lives within the overall medium of our personality." He adds that, "Each sub-personality has a style and a motivation of its own, often strikingly dissimilar from those of the others." (6) He quotes Assagioli, "We are not unified; we often feel that we are, because we do not have many bodies and many limbs, and because one hand doesn't usually hit the other. But, metaphorically, that is exactly what does happen within us. Several sub-personalities are continually scuffling: impulses, desires, principles, aspirations are engaged in an unceasing struggle."(7)

Discovering our sub-personalities through reflection gives us a way to gain a relatively clear picture of our inner life by taking stock of the various ways in which we look at life and by examining our behavior in various situations. It is helpful to name these constellations of traits or behaviors. For example, if a person devotes major energy, attempting to please everyone, including those who realistically don't play a significant role in the given person's life, this behavior pattern might be labeled *The Pleaser*.

Ferrucci notes that the ultimate aim of sub-personality work is getting to know our sub-personalities and hence increase of our sense of self. To the extent that this occurs, these different aspects of ourselves can experience greater integration. He adds that, "Awareness not only liberates, it also integrates."(8)

In Ferrucci's words, it is important to understand that sub-personalities can be thought of as "degraded expressions of the archetypes of higher qualities."(8) He notes that compassion can become self-pity, humor can become sarcasm. But the reverse can also be true. Self-pity can be elevated to compassion, sarcasm can become humor. When there is degradation from the higher states of consciousness, there is conflict. When there is an elevation of these sub-personalities, there can be movement toward unity. "Sub-personalities …are degradations or distortions of timeless qualities existing in the higher levels of the psyche. Ferrucci adds that "the compulsive seducer is a distant relative of love in its higher aspect; the obstinate sub-personality may be seen as a distortion of will."(9)

When we are able to recognize a sub-personality, it is important to step outside its behavior and observe it. In Psychosynthesis, this process is called dis-identification. The ultimate aim in sub-personality work is to increase one's sense of awareness of one's sub-personalities in order that a reintegration at a higher level can occur, free from the earlier distortions.

Dis-identification

From the perspective of Psychosynthesis, the relationship of the mind/body/emotion triad is seen as critical for human well-being.

This frame of reference attempts to give clarity to the essential unity of these three aspects of wholeness. The mind/body/emotion dimensions of our awareness are seen as important elements in the negotiations that are involved in choice. Assagioli speaks of the importance of dis-identification in healing. The process of dis-identification can be understood by recognizing that while we have a body, we are more than the summation of our body parts and functions. While we have emotions, we are more than our emotions. We have a mind, but we are more than our thoughts, fantasies, images. While we also have a spirit, we are more than spirit. When dis-dentification has been completed through reflective and meditative processes using relaxation and imagery, one is then associated to one's "more than" core essence, *The Center.* Here in the Center, according to Assagioli, one can get in touch with a source of wisdom/knowing that is associated with the Center. From this Center, through the imaginative visual processes, one can communicate with the mind/body/spirit aspects of oneself.

The Personal Self or the "I"

Psychosynthesis sees the Self as the most elementary and distinctive part of our being—its core. The core is of an entirely different nature from all the learned elements, such as physical sensations, feelings and thoughts, and thus can act as a unifying Center, directing these elements and bringing them into the unity of an organic wholeness. This Self or "I" is essential as the organizing Center and becomes known through discovery of what already is one's basic nature.

Ferrucci makes the point that "... the self can also be defined as the only part of us which remains forever the same." It "... remains the same in ecstasy and despair, in peace and turmoil, in pain and pleasure, and in victory or defeat."(10)

The Will

It is important to distinguish between will and will power. Ferrucci reminds us that will springs from the Center of our being, the Self, while will power is more related to sub-personalities. "When will springs from the Center, the will can express itself in many different ways and can be regarded as a constellation of inner events rather than a single, clear cut psychological manifestation. At times we realize the will in an instantaneous event, quick as a bolt of lightning, as in the case of a spontaneous act of courage or a sudden decision from which we cannot draw back. At other times, we may experience the will as a steady flow of strength, as when we concentrate our attention on some subject independently of outer distractions, or when we apply ourselves steadfastly to some project which we want to carry out regardless of the difficulties." He adds that the "the real function of the will is to direct, not to impose." The will acts from a proactive stance rather than a reactive one. The will, in tune with the higher unconscious, most often leads to positive, constructive behavior. Ferrucci adds, "... the will in its true essence can explain a host of human attainment, while its absence can account for legions of psychological disturbances. If understood in its proper perspective, the will is, more than other factor, the key to human freedom and personal power."(11)

Carroll:

When I took early retirement from public school teaching, I had intended to devote my self to writing, an activity that had proven meaningful and exciting in the past. The best way that I can describe this new direction was that I was being called to an activity that would tap into a level of creativity that I never dreamed possible. The major focus of this activity was to assist students, in many cases with no previous musical background, to create and produce their own operas. It was powerful to see changes in lives of individuals as they experienced previously untapped sources of energy. For many, it was truly a life-changing experience.Those involved were able to experience a source of higher energy, the place where willing occurs.

The central aspect of working with the will consists precisely in being conscious of what we do and how we do it. When the will is missing, the psychological space it should occupy is taken over by anguish, depression, resentment, confusion and rebellion.

The Training of the Will

Assagioli placed great emphasis on training the will. He saw this kind of "willfulness" as being related to discovering a sense of purpose. Such discovery is facilitated by becoming attuned, through meditation and reflection, to the higher or transpersonal self.

The mind or the intellect is crucial in "thinking through" alternative strategies that are consonant with the higher purpose. Once accomplished, it is important to choose and will a strategy that is in tune with our higher purposes as well as our feelings and cognitive resources.

Eugene:

I first met Virginia at an Alcohol Treatment Center. Her heavy drinking reflected an intense level of grief that she had not resolved following her husband's death. Once she began to resolve her grief-related issues, she chose to refocus on her excessive weight.

A highly visual person, she was invited to visualize that sub-personality which she had labeled the Hungry One and take it to a mountain top symbolizing the higher self. Having no difficulty visualizing this, she was then invited to dialogue with that part of her which was concerned with her body weight and seek validation of her expressed interest in changing her eating behavior. Her overweight body, often taxed through the overload of food, quickly gave approval to the plan.

She was then invited to discuss this proposition with her mind. There were plenty of intellectual reasons why a change in her eating behavior was very important. Again she gained her mind's approval for this change of behavior.

When she sought approval from the emotional aspect of herself, she was startled by the rapid and unequivocal veto. She realized for the first time why her long history of diets had so utterly failed. While she had managed to lose many pounds over the years, like many others she had regained those pounds, and then some, rather rapidly.

It became clear at that moment that the work of negotiating with the emotional aspects of this issue had not been resolved. Before we could continue to appropriately deal with dieting, other issues needed to be resolved, some of long standing, before a permanent change could be made.

Bringing Psychosynthesis to Life

To further illustrate the elements of Psychosynthesis as they occur in our lives, we share the following stories and thoughts.

Carroll:

I have a sub-personality which I call my workaholic. My workaholic was developed in my life when I was a boy growing up on a farm in north-central Ohio. I wanted to study piano. Boys did not study music. That was 'sissy; stuff. So as a small boy, to validate my manhood, I produced as much work in the field as any grown man. In return I received much praise and validation. Today, if I'm in need of affirmation, I am tempted to allow my workaholic to take charge of my life. It is important, however, that I go to my Center to examine this need for affirmation and to put this need into an appropriate perspective.

Sub-personalities are abstractions and provide a creative way of looking at our personality. They develop initially with good intentions. If those good intentions are expressed in limiting behaviors, however, they can work to one's disadvantage. Such sub-personalities can distort reality and come in conflict with each other. Intra-personal civil war among sub-personalities reflects the distress described by St. Paul: "That which I would do, I don't do. That which I wouldn't do, that I do." (**Romans 7:15**)

As one's search for wholeness unfolds, it is important to discover what one's various sub-personalities are intending to do, and what they want and need. Once their intentions are understood, ways to heal and re-integrate their limiting or twisted perspectives can be better understood. Using a process derived from Psychosynthesis, such sub-personalities (selves) can be up-dated and transformed to be more harmonious with one's essential core—*the Self*. The role of the Center is seen as an observer, integrator and synthesizer in this healing process. From the vantage point of this Center, sub-personalities are viewed from the perspective of their intentions in a sympathetic and accepting light even though they may be engaged in self-defeating behavior or in misdirecting energy. The goal, however, is to bring these sub-personalities into a harmonic whole.

Roberto Assagioli felt that Freud placed far too much emphasis on the suppression of that which is undesirable and socially not approved. He felt that too often we suppress the sublime within us. As one avenue to wholeness, our searching seeks strategies that are designed to attune and align the energies of the sub-personalities with that of the transpersonal or "higher" self.

A Multi-dimensional Approach

Our search for wholeness will examine some of the entry points that relate to a holistic health perspective. These entry points reflect the bio-physical, social-cultural, psycho-emotional, creative-intellectual and transpersonal-spiritual aspects of our being. Donald Tubesing, a Lutheran minister as well as a former director of a holistic wellness center, gave a stimulating workshop during the '70s in which he described human behavior in five dimensions: physical, social, emotional, intellectual and spiritual. In identifying and working with behavioral responses, he looked first at behavioral symptoms, then the causes and, finally, the remediation across these dimensions.

For example, if a child is not achieving intellectually, Tubesing would explore whether or not the child was receiving appropriate social support. He might question whether the child is receiving affirmation at home and at school or whether, or if, this child knows that he/she is valued. He would also raise questions about his or her physical environment. Is this student receiving adequate rest, appropriate nourishment and exercise? With the alarming increase of obesity, it is important that we examine the root causes of these physical concerns and develop multi-dimensional approach to holism.

Looking at the emotional dimension, Tubesing might question whether the child has a positive self-image or how the student feels about his/her contribution to the family, the classroom and to his or her peers.

Another question he might raise has to do with the spiritual/aesthetic dimension of their learning. Does he/she feel excitement and energy in the learning process and does this child feel meaning and some sense of connection with what is being presented?

Both of us will attempt to illustrate this multidimensional approach to wholeness and healing.

Eugene:

As a consultant to physicians, I have observed that more and more physicians are beginning to be aware that diagnosis and cure do not depend solely on analysis growing out of test tubes or elaborate laboratory or surgical procedures. If the entry point of health is biological-physical, it is not only critical to look at all of the factors that disturb the circulatory, respiratory or digestive systems, but also on non-biological-physical factors that may be contributing to symptoms. Medical treatment that focuses narrowly on the bio-physical 'cure' of an ulcer without paying attention to the associated social, emotional, educational or spiritual factors hardly leads to whole health.

A personal example illustrates the importance of the focusing on wholeness. Some years ago, my blood pressure was pushing the upper limits of normal. My weight was becoming excessive—forty pounds or so beyond my ideal weight. At the same time, I was allowing a growing practice to consume a vast amount of my energies, often in excess of 100 hours per week. From the framework of Psychosynthesis, a sub-personality labeled the workaholic or striver frequently pulled a coup and took over my integrative Center. During this 'driven' period, I felt exhausted and de-energized. When I would finally arrive home at late hours of the evening, I would be aware of a penetrating hunger even though I had 'wolfed down' more than a sufficient amount of food for my nutritional needs. I paid little attention to a balanced diet. No wonder the nocturnal refrigerator raids provided so little satisfaction other than a meek surrender to a strong impulse to eat.

The telling question was and is: which part of me was hungry? For what? I was clearly seeking nourishment that simply wouldn't be satisfied by the compulsive activity of the 'workaholic' who was still pushing and driving for even more performance. Clearly, this kind of hunger would not be satisfied by bread alone.

While my wife of nearly sixty years and I have strong commitments to each other, there have been communication blocks that we have not confronted forthrightly. Certainly this, as well as other factors, had to be faced holistically if the bio-physical concerns that related to my blood pressure were going to be dealt with effectively.

The entry point in dealing with my concern about physical health could have been psycho-emotional. Using this approach, the emphasis may well have been placed on the threats to my masculine adequacy experienced in the marriage. It could have easily focused on the fears I had experienced in terms of my approval needs, particularly in relation to my workaholic sub-personality.

Certainly the search for the early origins of deep-seated feelings of insecurity, related to emotional and social deprivation in my childhood, would provide a fertile ground for investigation. Unresolved conflicts from childhood may have emerged. Conflicts express themselves in the here and now. One clear example relates to the difficulty that I have had in dealing with anger. In my early, pietistic,'fundamentalistic' background, it was unacceptable to express or own anger. As a result, I learned to bury my anger feelings so deeply underground that I frequently am not directly in touch with them. All too often I have expressed such feelings indirectly in passive-aggressive ways.

How exciting it was to discover my angry sub-personality and by transforming its enormous energy to be able to put it to more creative use! It might even have effects such as lowering blood pressure.

A Creative-intellectual Approach

From the vantage point of Psychosynthesis, it is important to recognize the conscious as well as unconscious forces at work in human behavior, and their relationship to brain and intellectual functions.

While it is simplistic to speak of the functions of the right hemisphere of the brain being related to the affective domain, and the left hemisphere to the cognitive, this distinction is helpful in pointing out how sterile it is to explore the cognitive dimension without the affective, or to experience something without being concerned about its content. Distorted, partial effects grow out of emphasizing only one side (typically the left side) of cerebral functioning.

A generation of psychologists has struggled with the mysteries of how cognition occurs. While the mind and brain obviously are interdependent, they certainly are not one and the same. Many functions of the brain appear to occur at an unexplainable, seemingly pre-conscious level while we typically think of the mind functions as being conscious.

Carroll:

I'm aware that I am processing information in ways that I do not fully understand. Several years ago, my wife and I were in a struggle in our relationship. I thought about it much of the time, trying to find meaning in that struggle. I was working in my yard one afternoon when I stopped to watch a butterfly flutter by me and land on a branch of a tree, then quickly lift its wings and go its own way. Something connected at that point in my consciousness. I went inside the house and quickly penned the following poem:

Love, you are a butterfly
Waiting to break free.
The tiny threads
Which wrap your growing
Changing self
Are both a prison
And a place of security

Only you in your own time
Can break those threads
That broken
Allow your wings to spread
And lift you to thePetaled fragrance of eternity.

Why does Nature
With such delicacy
Create a formidable fortress
'Round your soul?
Is it that you are so fragile
That you must struggle
To find the strength to be?

How does the mind work in ways that such lines can come so quickly and easily? Something in my consciousness caused me to connect the stages of a butterfly with the struggle in a loving relationship. If one tries to help the butterfly out of its cocoon, it cannot fly. A loving relationship must be willing to face conflicts. One must work through the problems. We are often confronted with the delicate thread that holds mind and body together, and awed and terrified when we see cardiovascular problems occur. People who have been brilliant and articulate are severely incapacitated in a moment of time. How sad also to witness the gradual but permanent deterioration of mental faculties of persons who have experienced a gradual vascular "shut down" such as Alzheimer's Disease.

Many of us remember how vulnerable we felt when a young and vigorous president, and later his brother, was "cut down" by assassin's bullets. One moment there was keen conscious awareness; the next that awareness was gone. We momentarily shuddered as we considered the possibilities that these outstanding leaders could have survived biologically with their cognitive abilities destroyed.

Cognition is crucially related, although not exclusively, to linear thinking tasks such as mathematical calculations and systemic organizational tasks. The ability to "figure things out" is a highly valued and essential skill and clearly not the exclusive province of linear, rational thought.

An Interesting Speculation

We know that inspiration is present at innovative moments. In a small discussion group, Rollo May, a brilliant psychologist, described how, in a "stuck moment" during his doctoral studies, his whole research design was changed in a flash of insight that literally occurred between "one step and another" as he was walking to the subway. He suggests that this dynamic moment would not have occurred had he not been giving concerted attention to this problem.

During this same session, May also posited a very interesting hypothesis about people who are typically thought of as being on society's fringe. He suggests that these people often reflect, almost in a predictive sense, directions in which society is unconsciously beginning to move. If this hypothesis has merit, it may well be that "fringe people," whose behavior is often seen as unacceptable at a given moment, may in fact represent patterns of behavior that in a relatively short time will find conscious acceptance in the psyche of the social system.

A number of examples demonstrate the viability of this hypothesis. One can be drawn from the colonial period of our own history. In the period prior to the revolution, many of the colonists were loyal to the crown. On the other hand, those leaders who were offended by the actions of the king had an important impact on the history of what was to become the United States, not only in terms of the independence of the nation but in the independence of thought that is identified with the individual American.

The demise of apartheid in South Africa provides another example. Three decades ago Nelson Mandela was imprisoned for life for fomenting social change. No one then foresaw the day when a change in consciousness would ordain him to be the president of South Africa and herald a new day in their social system.

Gandhi, who spent a number of years in South Africa, became the father of a nation using a strategy that at one time was seen as ineffective. However, that non-violent approach to gaining power also brought about significant changes in consciousness. His example inspired Martin Luther King Jr. to lead a force producing immense change in the social system of the United States. Few would have dared to believe that the legal walls of segregation would fall so quickly.

Similarly, no one in the first century would have predicted that a non-credentialed teacher by the name of Jesus of Nazareth would so profoundly influence the world order.

It is interesting to ponder what role the Indians from the State of Chiapas, Mexico will play in bringing a new social order in Mexico. Or closer to home, if we assume some validity to May's hypothesis regarding people on the fringe, what is the meaning of the tension on the abortion question between those in the United States who strongly advocate the Right to Life and those who, with equal conviction, defend the Freedom of Choice perspective? A number of fiercely independent groups operate within this country. Is there meaning beyond the acts that may result in positive change or are they simply errant, self-serving groups?

This kind of integration appears to have profound implication for whole health. Biofeedback is one of the intriguing demonstrations of the willfulness that is involved in health promotion. This kind of potential is only beginning to be explored.

Much can be said for an educational approach to health. One of the propositions of holistic health is that the individual bears much of the responsibility for his/her healthful state, rather than relying on a colonial model where the "uninformed native" waits patiently and gratefully for the authority figure to give "doctor's orders" which when followed are intended to achieve some state of physical well-being.

The postulate presented in these pages points to the importance of individuals accepting the responsibility for their health and using the best consultants available to choose cognitively and willfully to be physically whole. These consultants represent a broad spectrum of traditional and non-traditional health care givers.

Another important dimension in holistic health is the social and cultural history that has forcefully shaped our values and attitudes about health and life. In his book, *Actualizing Therapy,* psychologist Everett Shostram quotes fellow-psychologist W. Crampton who points to four damaging patterns of health abuse that the average "macho" male acts out in a frantic effort to validate his masculinity: "1) He hides illness....2) He denies fatigue....3) He conceals emotions....4) He ignores injury."(12) This kind of cultural legacy, which was undoubtedly a response to strong survival instincts, can be seen through appreciative historical eyes, while at the same time reassessed in light of the hierarchy of needs that Abraham Maslow has articulated. Psychosynthesis, with its focus on the wants and needs of the sub-personalities, becomes a useful tool in exploring these early determinants of behavior in potentially reorienting and life-changing ways.

Don't Forget to Play

A lack of permission to play and to celebrate is powerfully rooted in our personal and cultural history.

Carroll:

Along with a dozen or so people who served as a support and reference group for Eugene in his Jesuit-sponsored Doctor of Ministry program, we devoted an entire weekend to the discovery of some of the dimensions related to play. Several of the group members, who tried to get inside the New Testament imagery of gaining access to the Kingdom of God by becoming a child, became painfully aware that they knew little about being children. Their cultural heritage had shaped them early in life into becoming miniature adults which limited them from engaging in uninhibited, spontaneous play. Some became aware that, like the Elder Son in the parable of the Prodigal Son, they had experienced few festivals in their lives.

Learning how to be children, how to celebrate, may indeed have profound implications for healthful living. Even though the ties of the extended and nuclear family weaken, the issue of how to relate to each other, how to be playful, how to validate each other's adequacy, will not go away. "No man is an island..." Our definition of community and how we act out that definition will be crucial in the search for wholeness.

Children acquire much of their language, concepts and skills through play. Their imaginations are free to flow. Much of their development, centered in loving, caring, and meaningful play, gives the child easy access to acquiring skills and understandings.

The Heart and Soul of it All

A final entry point into health which we wish to emphasize is the transcendent or spiritual. Such well-known authors as the American existential psychologist Rollo May and the Austrian neurologist and psychiatrist Viktor Frankl, among others, have written extensively about "loss of meaning" as being related to the anguish that the modern person experiences. This anguish will not be drowned out or lessened by the efficient hum of sophisticated computers on the information highway.

Karl Jung focused on human relationships to universal energies, suggesting that we are a part of all that lives. He spoke of universal wisdom, the wisdom of the ages, being located within the human psyche. (A discussion will follow on how blocked universal energies result in dis-ease.) More importantly, these same timeless energies, rooted in the universal and eternal, are crucial to the development of whole health.

From Another Perspective

Both Eastern and Western religions have focused on meditation as a tool to attune the searcher to wholeness and these universal energies. In the pages that follow, meditation will be presented as a major vehicle for the attunement of the "lower and higher selves." A look at the chapter titles will reveal that the entry points into whole health will be explored from different perspectives, including using a theological dimension. At the same time, this approach will focus on the psychological as well as physical dimensions of our lives.

While such words as confession, repentance, forgiveness and reconciliation are key words in any theological system, these concepts are not, by any stretch of the imagination, the sole domain of theology—East or West. They are in the very heart of the human experience and thus have a central role in many disciplines in the exploration of the human spirit. We will, without apology, move across academic disciplines in the use of these concepts in an attempt to see more clearly the meaning of our existence and the processes of healing through the use of these concepts.

Eugene:

Some years ago I was conducting a group psychotherapy session in a mental health center. After one particularly potent session, I was reflecting upon what had occurred. I suddenly realized that the ingredients of confession, repentance, forgiveness and reconciliation had been present, even though the participants had not approached the process in any particularly religious way.

On further reflection, it occurred to me that the journey from confession to reconciliation was a sequential process. Repentance, suggesting a change of priorities and a sense of willing, could not occur prior to the openness and emotional nakedness implied in confession. Similarly, the process of forgiveness could not be actuated without experiencing the confession and repentance. Reconciliation cannot occur prior to confession, repentance and forgiveness having occurred.

Switching on the Light

As we reflected on the process of change, of generating a new beginning, it occurred to us that there is a significant fallout or slippage between the act of confession and the act of repentance. Repentance is essentially a behavioral and attitudinal change, most often a "letting go" process, releasing behaviors that no longer fit. Rarely does repentance occur if confession has not taken place. There is truly the need, first, to be fully aware and to own the conditions in one's life and those things which one needs to change.

Repentance can be thought of as analogous to a light switch which acts to get the illumination process started. Forgiveness, then, is the electricity, the power creating supportive action, and a subsequent reconciliation is the light we so enjoy.

Clearly it is possible to make a confession and recognize the need for change without making the change itself. Those who have attempted, unsuccessfully, to change an ingrained behavioral pattern, such as over-eating, can attest to the validity of this assertion.

What does it mean to confess? Traditionally, the assumption has been made that confession impacts the "shadow side" of human existence. Theologians have also spoken of the "sins of omission" as well as the "sins of commission." In this context, "knowing to do good and doing it not" is seen as being sinful.

Beyond the negative connotation of confession, it is also necessary to confess and own one's strengths. There is abundant evidence suggesting that failure to validate one's strengths can lead to dysfunctional behavior in much the same way a muscle atrophies when it is not exercised. Jesus' parable of the unused talents, as reported in Matthew 25:14-30, points to the importance of using our strengths in stewardship terms.

Eugene:

As a child in elementary school, I grew up with the image and attitude that I was sub-standard both intellectually and in my ability to relate to people. Predictably I functioned badly in school and in developing social graces.

I remember how shocked I was when I received my very first academic grade of A. It was in high school typing class. This proved to be the first 'crack of light' in seeing myself differently. I was much too timid to make an open confession of gifts that were inside me, even to myself. Still, this was the first moment of awareness that I remember acknowledging to myself that the myths I held about myself might not be true.

Carroll:

After many years of coordinating an elementary music education program, which was personally very rewarding, my position was discontinued. I was reassigned to the position of principal of an alternative school, grades K-8. After two years I realized that much of my energy was consumed by things which did not feed me personally. I recognized that many other individuals could do that work. I was also aware that there was work to be done which I was capable of doing and which was more unique to my abilities. I chose to take early retirement and then went back into the district and worked pro bono, doing for children and teachers that which also fed me.

Shostrom has focused on the importance of accepting and disclosing the emotional polarities of love-anger and strength-weakness if there is to be congruency among our feeling, thinking and being selves.(13) For us, the question is not centered around whether or not to confess, but rather on how voluntary and authentic the confession is to be. Much has been written about involuntary confession that is evidenced in such behavior as slips of the tongue and body language at odds with the spoken word. Authentic and willful confession is part of the dynamic process that leads to integration and wholeness, while involuntary confession is de-energizing.

Feelings of guilt have often been associated with the confession of "shadow-like" behavior. In his book, *Guilt and Grace*, Paul Tournier, a Swiss psychiatrist, has attempted to differentiate between true and false guilt. He points out that false guilt is culturally-induced guilt, such as the violation of societal taboos or social constraints. Real guilt, on the other hand, is related to value-oriented guilt; a guilt where there "is the genuine consciousness of having betrayed an authentic standard."(14) False guilt needs to be dealt with in the counseling room while the real or authentic guilt needs to be dealt with in the spirit of repentance. He further implies that, historically, the Church has tended to assume that all guilt was real and repentance was imperative while secular psychology has assumed that guilt is false and culturally-imposed and needed to be dealt with in the therapy room. Tournier feels that it is essential to make this important distinction between false and real guilt before devising a strategy for dealing with guilt.

From the bio-physical perspective, stepping on the weighing scales may induce feelings of guilt, in part because of the growing awareness of the relationship of weight to optimum health. However, it can also serve as an invitation to go on to the next step in the process, namely, repentance, the initiation of a change in behavior. It should be noted that confession, however valid, does not always lead to repentance, nor repentance to change. The dropout rate is great at this crucial point in the process.

Often the fragile attempt to repent and change behavior gets undermined by the insensitivity of persons who are part of one's crucial support group. For example, many people who have attempted to stop smoking have felt sabotaged by associates who 'blow smoke in their faces' in the very early part of the battle, when the unadjusted blood levels are screaming for nicotine. On the other hand, while the sensitivity of a caring person or persons is necessary, it is not a sufficient condition for change.

In the language of Psychosynthesis, integration takes place at several levels. A sub-personality represents the pseudo-core that has attracted and synthesized various personality elements to give body or expression to the sub-personality. Following this model, there are within us a number of sub-personalities which await a higher order synthesis. When achieved, the result is a harmonious expression of the self-actualizing human being.

We propose the following hypothesis: the higher the congruence or integration among the sub-personalities, coupled with the congruence and support of external groups, the more likely that repentance and change in behavior will occur and be sustained.

Internal and external blocks (incongruities) to repentance are discussed below. We will attempt to illustrate those conditions that promote integration and changed behavior in the various sub-categories of whole health. We emphasize that behavior en route to being changed needs to be practiced, much as a beginning piano student must mechanically place and repeatedly move fingers correctly on the keyboard before this behavior becomes fully integrated.

When Not to Hang On

Assuming authentic confession has occurred, followed by repentance, and the early signs of changed behavior have emerged, what are the blocks to forgiveness? What facilitates the "lifting of the heaviness" when the real thing (forgiveness) occurs?

Forgiveness, in these terms, is the working through of the struggle that was initiated at the time of confession and repentance. There is a sense in which forgiveness can be seen as expansive in that forgiveness leads to integration and wholeness. This kind of integration is renewing and begins to resemble the dynamic energy that is present in the universe.

Forgiveness has intra-personal dimensions as well as interpersonal and supra-personal elements. Forgiveness cannot be present on demand. It is always a gift: a manifestation of grace. When the processes of grace have been fully experienced through confession, repentance and forgiveness, there predictably will be a sense of fullness or unity with oneself and one's neighbor, as well as a sense of relatedness to the universe. New life occurs within the individual.

Of course, to begin the healing process, it is necessary to experience the phenomenon of grace. Grace is not earned. Rather it is a state freely given. It is acceptance without condition. In such a state one enjoys the highest levels of trust and is free to take those significant risks with which growth is associated. Such a state of being is a fundamental base to the forming of a lasting community—the family, a church, a social club or other groupings which bring like-minded people together. Not only is grace essential to the beginning of the healing process; it must likewise be present throughout the larger growth process.

Looking Forward to Change

We end our discussion of the process leading to wholeness by posing the following questions. What are some of the personal concerns which confront all of us? (+++) How do we take this process toward wholeness into our encounter with the future? (+++) Is there a predictable direction in which our world, our universe is headed? (+++)

As you study and experience the exercises, we suggest you apply these processes to your own life. We also encourage you to find a significant other with whom you might share your responses. It is in the sharing of these processes that we have been able to draw upon those energies which inspirit us and help us meet our daily demands.

Chapter 2
NATURE OF GRACE
It's Amazing

Listen well to what I cannot say.
Help me believe that what's unknown
Contains a special beauty
That may
Help me accept myself
In the midst of my vulnerability.
[Carroll Rinehart]

JOHN NEWTON, who became a Captain of a sailing vessel, was heavily involved in shipping slaves to the Americas. He apparently had all of the characteristics of a hard-driving and drinking seaman who never missed a chance to "make a buck" regardless of the wreckage of human lives along the way. In mid-life, John Newton had a profound conversion and eventually became an Anglican minister and played a significant role in influencing the British Parliament to stop the human savagery of the slave trade. He is best known, however, for his song, *Amazing Grace*. That grace, from his perception, was instrumental in changing his world-view and the values that informed his actions during the second half of his life. What follows are two of Newton's verses:

'Twas grace that taught my heart to fear,
and grace my fears relieved;
how precious did that grace appear
the hour I first believed.

Through many dangers, toils and snares,
I have already come;
'tis grace hath brought me safe thus far,
and grace will lead me home.

Philip Yancey, in his book, *What's So Amazing About Grace,* tells of Bill Moyers' documentary film on the hymn Amazing Grace which included a scene filmed in Wembley Stadium in London. He states that various musical groups had gathered to celebrate the end of apartheid in South Africa. While most groups were rock bands, the promoters also scheduled an opera singer, Jessye Norman, as the closing act.

Yancey describes the documentary film as shifting from scenes of an unruly crowd in the stadium and Jessye Norman being interviewed. "… twelve groups like Guns 'n' Roses have blasted the crowd through banks of speakers, riling up fans already high on booze and dope. The crowed yells for more curtain calls, and the rock groups oblige. Finally the time comes for her to sing. A single circle of light follows Norman, a majestic African-American woman wearing a flowing African dashiki, as she strolls onstage. No backup band, no musical instruments, just Jessye. The crowd stirs, restless. Few recognize the opera diva. A voice yells for more Guns 'n' Roses. Others take up the cry. The scene is getting ugly.

Alone, a capella, Jessye Norman begins to sing, very slowly:

Amazing grace, how sweet the sound, that saved a wretch like me! I once was lost but now am found, was blind but now I see.

A remarkable thing happens in Wembley Stadium that night. Seventy thousand raucous fans fall silent by her aria of grace. By the time Norman reaches the second verse, "Twas grace that taught my heart to fear, And grace my fears relieved…" the soprano has the crowd in her hands. By the time she reaches the end of the third verse, "Twas grace has brought me safe thus far, And grace will lead me home," several thousand fans are singing along, digging far back in the nearly lost memories for words they heard long ago.

Jessye Norman later confessed that she had no idea what power descended on Wembly Stadium that night. I think I know. The world thirsts for grace. When grace descends, the world falls silent before it."(15)

Grace is often identified as favor, mercy, or theologically as a form of divine forgiveness which cannot be earned but is unconditionally given. Grace has a relationship to energy. It connotes conditions which must exist before energy can be released and made available to support growth. When grace is present, there is a sense of direction that is present even in the midst of conflict. When that grace is lacking, we tend to experience conflicting forces within us, such as resentment or hurt. It is difficult, in such moments, to be fully present to ourselves and the world about us.

Energy is the most pervasive force in the universe. Electrons, neutrons, protons and other sub-atomic particles which compose atoms have an energy relationship with each other. In addition, atoms themselves are in a state of motion, as is true of all living matter. The contemporary String Theory states that beyond electrons, neutrons, and protons, there is energy. We will hold that this energy, which is universal, is not available to us until grace or unconditional acceptance is present.

Grace is like a river channel accumulating energy as it moves from its headwaters on its way to the sea. The drops of water which make up the mighty river, like grace, do not have to earn their right to be there. Their place just is! Grace is freely given, freely received; it can never be demanded, it is unconditional in character.

Graceful Relationships

Have you ever noticed that in some social situations you are drawn to certain people who seem to accept you? (+++) Conversely, do you avoid people who let you know that you will have to meet certain standards in order to gain their approval? (+++)

Describe an experience in which everything felt so right that you were willing to surrender yourself into that experience. (+++) Remember a time when you felt a high sense of personal worth; when you were lifted to a higher level of human experience. (+++)

For many people such moments are associated with creative

acts which contain transcending qualities. Reflect on situations and people with whom you feel most fully accepted. (+++) What do you do to create the opportunity to be with the unconditional acceptors? (+++) Now reflect on situations and people with whom you feel you must meet their expectation in order to be acceptable. How do you then redirect the relationship toward such conditional acceptors? (+++)

We like to be with those that accept us unconditionally. How do we become graceful in ungraceful situations? How can we be graceful when conditions are imposed on the relationship?

Eugene:

While serving as pastor of a new congregation, one member was a perfectionist who held his own high values and standards. In the beginning there was a cordial relationship. As this relationship deteriorated, and became increasingly ungraceful, I began to interpret this rejection as not meeting his values. I soon became immobilized.

One distinct memory I have is that, when I began my sermons, he would turn his face toward the wall and would avoid any eye contact. I allowed this action to condition what I had to say. Frequently I was at loss on how to proceed. These tensions continued throughout our relationship. The question is: What could I have done to change the conditions of acceptance? What could I have done to introduce grace into that relationship? (+++)

Moving Toward Gracefulness

Carroll:

She was a seven year old child living in an economically and socially depressed area of the city. I was to learn of her oppressive home life. When I first saw her she had her head on the desk with no response to what was happening in the classroom.

I began the classroom sessions with some silly songs accompanied by exaggerated movement. I made it a point to invite her into the activity and gently made physical contact with her. When she made her first move and responded, I affirmed her response.

In the weeks to follow she became more open, even choosing to give me hugs. I was always careful to affirm her. Meanwhile the children completed their opera of 'The Three Little Pigs.' Then, to my surprise, she volunteered to audition for each character in the story, standing very close beside me, making physical contact.

Her openness grew. In the fourth week of our project, upon seeing me enter the school campus, she came running to me and gave me a big hug. On the day of the performance she came rushing up to me and asked, 'Is there anything I can do to help you?'

I had begun to work with her to achieve an intellectual objective but before that could be accomplished she had to experience grace by being unconditionally accepted just as she was—socially, emotionally, physically and spiritually.

Growth requires certain basic pre-conditions. Individuals must be able to release themselves into experiences and relationships. Our generative energies must be free to flow. Most significant things in our lives cannot be predicted and planned with precision. We are best served by seizing the moments and growing through them often not knowing where they will lead us. If we are willing to move beyond our perception of vulnerability and take action in the face of uncertainty, we may truly be moving toward wholeness. One's willingness to risk is proportional to the levels of trust one experiences. The more one is known and accepted, the greater the level of trust which can develop.

When Passion Begins to Fade!

Too many lives are filled with experiences in which the excitement for work or tasks has become dulled. Energy is dissipated. A job, once filled with challenge, becomes routine and the zest for the work is lost. The challenge for growth is no longer present. Even play may become meaningless.

Schools are filled with programs so predictable that there is little excitement present for students or teachers. All that is left is to fill in the blanks. Even the way the blanks are arranged is predictable.

Many marriages also become predictable, each spouse expecting and predicting how the other will respond. What was once a most intimate experience, where invitations were abundant and both parties were fully present, is now overly familiar. It becomes a game, each player playing according to the prescribed, unspoken, but understood rules. One day, the awareness emerges that the relationship has become static. The enthusiasm and aliveness that was once present no longer exist. A 'death' has occurred. Grieving for what has been lost follows.

Consider the energy contained in high voltage power lines. Sent energy is a strong force for enabling growth, creating efficiencies and facilitating productivity. However, when such power lines are downed, then energy can become a destructive and fearful force. Reports of spousal and child abuse, and conflict between individuals are examples of the explosive and faulty use of energy.

Eugene:

I have been fortunate in that I have enjoyed the jobs in which I have been involved—with one significant exception. It was in a work setting that I valued but I came to dislike the particular dimensions of my expected job performance. I simply didn't believe in what I was doing. I could find no source of inspiration or creativity. When I announced my frustration to a supervisor, his advice was to do anything that would ensure the money on this specific grant being renewed.

It became increasingly clear that I had accepted the job at the urging of a valued friend and mentor. He worked in the same setting but in an entirely different role. Both of us wanted to be in the same vicinity in order to facilitate some common work goals that were not part of my assigned task.

I still remember with some pain how restless I became. I could hardly wait for the weekend. When Sunday evenings arrived, I would began to pace as I anticipated facing a job that I came to truly dislike.

It was Friday afternoon when I read the institution's newsletter. It quoted a few lines from Gilbran's essay on work. The line that forcefully 'jumped out of the page' at me went: 'If you cannot work with love but only with distaste, it is better that you should leave your work and sit at the gate of the temple and take alms from those who work with joy.' It was a graceful and liberating moment. I knew I could no longer stay. It was with a sense of great relief that I gave myself permission to leave.

An Opportunity to Reflect!

Take a moment to reflect on some relationship (a marriage, a job, a friendship). Identify the level of freshness in the relationship. (+++) Be aware of where, in the relationship, the energy may have diminished or evaporated. What has become too predictable, too routine? (+++) Are there areas of freshness and newness? (+++) Where would you like freshness and novelty to exist? (+++) What can you do to facilitate the introduction of that freshness and novelty? (+++)

When You're Stuck!

Creative energies can get blocked in our society when people get caught up in unhealthy attitudes about their physical beings; for example, being unwilling to accept their bodies. By thinking that social acceptance has something to do with being a perfect "10" physically, we reject our bodies and squander energies by regretting that we don't measure up.

Eugene:

Some years ago I saw a young female client who was so physically attractive that I wouldn't have been surprised had she announced she had been in a beauty pageant. Hence, I was caught completely off guard when early in the interview she lamented about how ugly she was. Puzzled by her comment, I inquired where and how she had derived that perception of herself.

I was astonished by her response. She pointed to a tiny blemish on her face which was barely noticeable. I learned that she spent hours in front of a mirror examining this blemish with a magnifying glass. She had made this tiniest of flaws into a disabling condition for herself.

Societal norms dictating beauty, both feminine and masculine, can result in people punishing their bodies. In such circumstances individuals lose touch with the reminder of poets and theologians that we are the "temple of God" and miss moments of grace regarding the uniqueness of our physical beings. It is important that we don't surrender to the advertising industry the right to define what beauty is and thereby miss the profound imagery that we are made in the image of our Creator.

Reflections

Are there things about you physically that you reject? (+++) Are you aware of why you hold these attitudes? (+++) What about you are you willing to share with others? About what are you willing to be most open? (+++) What do you most like about yourself? (+++) How does your perception about yourself affect your relationships with others? (+++)

Grace Filled Experiences

Risk is often a part of growth. Through risk we can determine the levels of trust that exist with the significant others in our lives. As one risks, careful note should be made of how the experience is received by the other person. We make the following hypothesis: the more open and affirming the reception, the greater the opportunity to risk even more in subsequent encounters.

Adding to Assagioli's imagery of sub-personalities in Psychosynthesis, we have described sub-personalities as being something like members of a family that reside within us. They exist because at some point in time they served a most valued function. As parts of us, they monitor all our behaviors, giving us feedback on how we are doing and what we should be doing. External feedback from people and events supports our own internal dialogue which can facilitate, challenge or inhibit our functioning. That is, when external feedback is congruent with our internal dialogue, our personal response is reinforced. For example:

1) “A” thinks he’s slow and inept and gets criticized by his boss. “A” feels hurt, more anxious and becomes slower and more inept (congruent messages to inhibited functioning).

2) “A” thinks well of himself and is praised by his boss. “A’s” positive attitude is expanded (congruent messages facilitating functioning).

3) “A” thinks poorly of self but gets praise from the boss for a job well-done (incongruent messages challenging “A’s” self-perception and opening the possibility for growth on “A’s” part).

4) “A” thinks he’s done a good job but gets criticized by his boss whose standards are excessive (incongruent messages challenges “A’s” self perception, opening the possibility for “A” to mistakenly internalize his bosses perception. The result? Inhibited functioning.

Reflections

Think for a moment about your internal dialogue that helps you in decision-making and action. Which parts of you (sub-personalities) contribute to making decisions and determining action? (+++) How would you describe these “sub-personalities?” What labels (names) would be most fitting for each of them? (+++)

The role of what in Pychosynthesis is called the Center is to facilitate coordination between the sub-personalities.

Gracelessness

People often allow conformity to norms to obscure larger issues which give greater purpose and meaning to life. Our educational system has programmed us to believe that performance on test scores has to do with our level of intelligence and ability to achieve in society. However, the only thing we know for sure from test scores is how well students can follow instructions and deal with bits and pieces of information. Such is hardly the essence of intelligence. The importance of achievement in test-taking can become so dominant that we fail to take note of those moments when a learner can make a significant leap forward in areas of his or her own interest and ability.

In our discussion of conditional and unconditional relationships, we have stressed the impact of each kind of relationship upon the development of individuals, and upon their ability to respond to their fullest potentials. When grace is present we set the stage for the empowerment of each other.

Reflections

In what ways do you feel a lack of freedom to explore or do things on your own? (+++) What contributes to that feeling? (+++) What would you need to do to experience greater freedom? (+++)

Eugene:

Gracelessness occurs when meaningful dialogue is missing. Such is exemplified when people 'fire their volleys' and then disappear. I remember performing a marriage ceremony on the beautiful grounds of a well-known lodge. The event had all the ingredients for a joyous occasion. The bride looked lovely in her traditional wedding gown. Family and friends had come from great distances to be at this festive event.

Some of the family members, well-intentioned no doubt, were uptight during the rehearsal. The rehearsal dinner that followed was more like a command performance than a celebration.

I typically conduct the wedding ceremony without any props or notes. Inadvertently, at one point, I used the wrong first name of the bride. Recognizing this error, I made it a point to repeat the bride's correct first name several times during the ceremony.

Following the ceremony the bride's brother made it a point to sullenly state that he hoped God would forgive me for my mistake because he never would.

He failed to recognize that the wedding was a celebration. He had seen it as a performance. Family and friends had gathered to witness a most important event. He focused so much attention on a flaw in the ceremony that he missed the larger celebratory event. In the future, when he thought of his sister's wedding, in all probability he would tune into my minor error. He likely would continue to miss the gracefulness of that joyous experience long after the ceremony.

High standards carried to an extreme of perfectionism can be a form of gracelessness.

Gracefulness

The quality of a relationship does affect how one engages in the human encounters that will follow. If the relationship is conditional, the tendency is to defend oneself and not be fully available to the potential that a given experience might offer.

Why is grace important? Like the set designer for a theatrical production, grace provides the setting for and becomes an important part of our growing and being. It is a part of every scene in the drama of life. Scenes filled with such things as evil, rage, deceit, and violence are reminders of the consequences when grace is not present.

Grace begins as unconditional acceptance and provides the context for a change process. Grace is experienced when one is freely granted acceptance accompanied by elements of mercy and clemency. It is experienced as the unmerited love and favor of God toward people. It dignifies and honors the individual.

Eugene:

It was during my mother's extended illness and subsequent death that my siblings and I were richly blessed by the graceful actions of a cousin. My siblings and I were all living in different geographical locations from my parents and each other. Except for trying to be attentive as we could by telephone, and an occasional visit, none of us was able to be present to monitor the day-to-day needs of either my mother, who was in a nursing home, or my father, who was living in an assisted-living retirement center.

It was a cousin whom I barely knew who took them 'under her wing' and attended to many of their needs. During the weeks following, first, my father's death, she went the 'second mile' and much more in caring for my mother who was in the final stages of Alzheimer's disease prior to her own subsequent death.

Even though she and her husband were in the middle of harvesting large fields of grain, a very demanding time for farmers, she eloquently hosted our family who had gathered from different parts of the country for the two services of celebration. She provided a wonderful western Nebraska style dinner the evening that we gathered for this event. She quickly dismissed our reluctance to accept her invitation during this very busy time as her gift of ministry to us. I learned that she and her husband, for whom farming was a major business, attempted to live out their life performing gracious acts of service.

Tenacity

Grace is enhanced by one's willingness to persevere. It is an outward, visible sign of commitment. How often have we failed to experience renewal because we were so unsure of the possibilities for change that we prematurely gave up? Commitment to follow through was missing.

Carroll:

Winnie was a fifth-grade teacher. In her class was a young boy who seemed unable to read. Throughout the year Winnie did everything she knew to effect improvement in this student's reading ability. Nothing worked. The end of the year came and neither she nor the young boy had experienced any success in the program.

Winnie went to the boy's mother and asked if she (Winnie) might take the boy home with her for the summer. She proposed that she would work with him there on a one-to-one basis. Permission was granted and Winnie bought two round trip bus tickets for their two thousand mile trip. On their journey, they worked on reading skills. No reading gains were made. Throughout the summer they worked. Still the boy made no gains.

Then it was time for the return trip and, again, they resumed the work together. Still, he gave no evidence of learning. Between Tulsa and Oklahoma City, during a break in their studies, Winnie asked the boy some questions about his father. This story unfolded: The young boy loved his father very much. They played together every moment available to them. Then the father got a sales job that took him away from home. The weekend reunions were wonderful. Between times there were letters from the father, letters that carried wonderful images of his father, letters that kept alive that very special feeling. Mother would rush to the mailbox and open the letters. Together they would share those moments.

One day mother rushed to the mail box, opened the letter and they sat down to share. This time the father said he would not be coming home. He had found another woman with whom he wanted to share his life.

As Winnie and the boy talked about the letter, the boy reasoned that if his mother had not been able to read the letter, then his father would still be with them, so real was the power of the written word. Winnie helped him understand what had happened. She explained that his inability to read had nothing to do with his father and their relationship. With that misconception eliminated, the boy was released from his reading block. By the time they arrived home, he was reading.

Winnie's belief in and care for the boy caused her to make an extraordinary commitment. She certainly went the extra mile in offering the boy her time and compassion. Moreover, she had been willing to confront him with the important essence of his story. With a new understanding he had been released, freed to resume growing and learning.

Where was the grace in this relationship? (+++) Certainly the teacher's investment of time and personal energy is an example of grace and tenacity. Many of us are where we are because, somewhere, a special person believed in us so much that s/he would not give up on us.

Carroll:

In a music education workshop, teachers were describing the significant people who had helped shape their lives. One teacher, with a sense of radiance, described her clarinet teacher. She described qualities that seemed oppressive, inflexible, demanding, almost uncaring. Another person in the group asked, 'How can you say he is significant, when that man seems to be the opposite of all the other qualities we have been describing?' The teacher quickly replied, 'He is the one person in my life who believed in me so much that he would not accept anything but my very best.' In that relationship she had experienced a quality of grace-filled caring that transcended all the demands he had placed upon her. That caring atmosphere her teacher had provided made significant growth possible for her.

Reflections

Who has cared about you so much that s/he would not give up? (+++) About whom have you cared enough that you would not give up on her/him? (+++) What has been the result of your commitment? (+++) What were the surprises? (+++)

Experiencing Grace

The ability to grow, to respond fully, to become a whole person is enhanced when grace is present. Grace is experienced when there is no need to modify or deny what is. Grace is present when one is at peace within oneself, when there is a sense of harmony among our sub-personalities. One is truly centered when grace is abundantly present.

Grace permits one to move freely from one sub-personality to another; that is, from a playful child to a nurturing parent to a rational thinker. These states are cooperative, harmonious and reflect congruent actions and interactions with others.

From the Psychosynthesis perspective, grace is a tapping into the Universal energies. These energies flow through the higher self to our Center and into the sub-personalities. It permits harmony and a possibility for a free flow between the various levels of consciousness. The following diagram illustrates this pattern of flow which provides grace-full experiences and wholeness:

UNIVERSAL ENERGIES

Higher Self/Soul
Life Qualities: Love, Truth, Beauty, Justice, Wholeness
Center (I)
Sub-Personalities: Workaholic, Playful Child, Pleaser, Adventurer, Perfectionist
(And a host of other internal children)

A lack of grace can become immobilizing. The following anecdote illustrates how inner grace (self acceptance) is also necessary to experience freedom. The lack of development of life qualities such as love, truth, beauty, justice, faith, and wholeness, often results in misdirected behavior, whether at an inter-personal, a larger community or an international level. These life qualities have rarely been transmitted except through the arts and the humanities and through significant personal relationships.

Carroll:

In my later years in public education I was a principal of an alternative school. The school was selected to participate in a national Dance-in-the-Schools program. This necessitated that I travel with a teacher from my school to Duke University to attend dance education workshops. During the day we did warm-ups and some dance work with some of the finest dance teachers in the country. In the evening we were treated to wonderful dance programs by some of the nation's great dance companies. Following the evening dance programs there were opportunities for recreational disco dancing, which was popular at the time.

As I stood watching others disco dance, a part of me was envious of their freedom to move. Then I was invited by Shirley Ririe (of the Salt Lake City based Ririe-Woodbury Dance Company) to join her on the dance floor. With great fear and trembling I stepped onto the floor. Suddenly my critical judge called my attention to the fact that I was dancing with a great dancer. Within moments I could hardly move one foot in front of the other. I was immobilized!

Two things followed. I confessed my discomfort to Shirley and internally acknowledged to myself that any movement on my part would be an improvement. From Shirley I sensed only acceptance of myself as a person. When the next piece of music began, I was released into it fully. With unrestrained movements we responded to the rhythms and the form of the music. Grace was present. I was able to engage fully in the play at hand.

When you've been to the mountain! ! !

Our pondering the essence of gracefulness and associated phenomenon has led us to conclude that grace is inseparably associated with generative energy. It points to the conditions which exist before energy can be released and made available.

One of the antecedent conditions is a hunger or longing for change. Significant change typically implies a great deal of risk. The weighing of such risks may be accompanied by fear and trepidation. If fear and trepidation dominate and immobilization follows, old patterns become more ingrained. Then, there is little chance that much of a creative experience will follow. If, however, the awareness of a hunger becomes so intense and our dissatisfaction with the way our life is being experienced becomes so intolerable that the "stones will cry out" if action isn't taken, then the experience of grace is not far away. The intensity of this kind of experience makes the risk of inaction almost unthinkable. Countless Christian martyrs reached such a state of readiness where they were required to take action in the face of death. Grace enabled martyrs to go to their deaths singing hymns of triumph while considering themselves privileged to die for something in which they believed so strongly.

Martin Luther King, Jr. apparently entered the struggle for

freedom and human rights reluctantly. Rosa Parks, sitting in the 'inappropriate' area of the bus, refused to move back behind the initial designated section filled with white people; in fact, more space was needed for them to be seated. Her refusal prompted the white driver to over-react and a movement was launched.

King, who was busily involved in completing a demanding doctoral program, purportedly intended to make only a token response to the "incident." As the dramatic events began to unfold, however, he was impelled to act. His life may have been simpler had he not been so impelled, but he had been 'called.' After he had "been to the mountain," even the threat of death did not hold him back from carrying out this calling.

If grace is seen as a triggering action or a means to releasing energy, then action, which upsets the established order of things can be grace-filled. Jesus' angry encounter with the temple money changers is a vivid example. Jesus undoubtedly experienced a tremendous surge of physical energy as he upset the money changing tables and scolded: "You have made the house of prayer a den of thieves."

Longing for change, which can be initially experienced as a kind of emptiness, often exists at an unconscious or preconscious level of awareness. A hunger-based, grace-filled trigger resulting in decisive action can come as something of a surprise. High energy, life-changing experiences may seem to occur suddenly and appear compulsive. Some hunger, however, may remain largely suppressed and unidentified until some final straw causes a break-through and action is taken.

All of us can cite examples of people who were willing to "lay down their lives for others" in grace-filled moments. We will not easily forget the gracefulness of the middle-aged man who survived the airline crash into the icy waters of the Potomac just before Christmas of 1981. In a position to be rescued, he gave the life line to another and perished before the helicopters returned. It is probable that his selfless act was actually associated with other moments of gracefulness reflecting his life values.

How much are you willing to risk?

Antecedents in addition to risk and longing must be present before energy can be triggered. High-rollers at the gambling casinos obviously take a lot of chances. However, "putting it on the line" in such distorted forms represents pathological functioning that can result in devastation and brokenness.

Violent behavior, enacted in the name of a worthy cause, is antithetical to grace. For example, the intense struggles centered around abortion issues often seem utterly lacking in grace. It is easy to see that extreme behaviors in any situation are counter-productive to change and growth. Killing the doctors who serve pro-choice clinics can hardly be seen as graceful acts. It can be argued that little difference exists between the shocking actions of a Mr. Hill (who killed a physician in his attempt to spare the unborn), and the Middle East Muslim and Jewish extremists who, in the name of God, kill those who hold different views. It is important to remember that whenever violence is committed, in any form, grace cannot be present.

Putting it on the line

Risking behavior that results in high levels of energy must be solidly grounded in values that address the essential existential questions of life's meaning and purpose. The ancient Hebrew prophet Micah underscored the value of loving justice and mercy. As noted earlier, proponents of Psychosynthesis identify the universal qualities of life as love, truth, beauty, justice, faith and wholeness. In some measure, these qualities need to be present before grace can occur. Grace becomes a means of experiencing these life qualities at ever-deeper levels.

How then, can we help create an atmosphere where grace can abound? A sense of being present to what is taking place, and being fully open to an experience, is a crucial ingredient. Such presence may be reflected in non-demanding ways; it may also be experienced as a confrontation. The following story is illustrative of such a confrontation.

Eugene:

A close friend and clergy colleague was experiencing a great deal of difficulty with his back and physical mobility. His physician had tentatively diagnosed his condition as a form of arthritis. He was of the opinion that decreasing mobility would likely continue. During an informal fellowship gathering of clergy and their spouses, my friend shared this prognosis. One by one his friends shared their dismay and their feelings of sympathy over his unfortunate state. Another valued friend, however, feeling uncomfortable about what was being said, sensed that something didn't ring true. He finally spoke to the person receiving these condolences: 'David, you'll probably have the arthritis as long as you need it.'

David reported that he initially felt angry and hurt by this confrontation. After a sleepless night, however, he recognized the truth in what his friend had had the courage to share. Subsequently he was able to let go of that which had been crippling him. In sharing his story, David stated that the confrontation had been far more helpful and grace-filled than all of the other well intended, supportive remarks.

Risking. Being Vulnerable

Early in the developmental process, children assertively announce that they 'can do it themselves.' Deeply rooted in our heritage is the myth of independence. It is as American as apple pie to feel that "I can do it on my own without help from anyone." This need often sets up the conditions that make it difficult for us to ask for help.

This is especially true for men who find it difficult to acknowledge need and weakness and ask for help. Grace often begins to flow, however, following such an acknowledgment when we allow others to minister to us. When we share our pain, our sense of failure, our fears, the moments when we experience a crisis of adequacy, we can open the gates of grace.

The late Reverend Dewane Zimmerman, a United Methodist minister and friend, reminded us that we experience our "growing edge" at the point where we are most vulnerable. At the edge of our vulnerability is the place where we are most real. It can be valuable to examine graceful moments and the grace-filled people who have blessed our lives in times of distress, need and vulnerability. Such recollections can be instrumental in allowing us to reconnect and re-experience the significance of those life-changing moments.

Reflections

Identify those people who have left a telling mark of grace on your life, perhaps in an unsuspecting moment? (+++) Think about how they have influenced your life. (+++)

Being off balance

Earlier we stated that grace is the channel through which energy flows. This channel can become blocked so that the expression of grace is thwarted. Assagioli seems to suggest that blocks of energy occur when people forget who they are in their totality and over-identify with a part of themselves, a sub-personality.

Eugene:

If I become over-identified with a pleaser sub-personality, I can become so concerned about pleasing those around me that I compromise who I really am. To illustrate: Suppose I'm conducting a consultation session with a hospital patient at the request of a referring physician. If I become so concerned about pleasing the referring physician that I forget to tune-in to the patient, I've not only short-changed the patient and the physician, but myself as well. In such a circumstance I will not be fully present to the patient and the channels of grace are likely to become clogged.

Keeping it all in balance

To the degree that we are able to be centered and in tune with our God-like essence, to that degree we are, also, likely to be in the flow of energy. From this internally centered locus, we can view aspects of ourselves, for example, the pleaser sub-personality, in a more integrated, compassionate and empathic light. From an integrated perspective, the pleaser sub-personality, under the direction of the Center, can release some of the distortion that has accumulated from a host of life experiences. In addition, we can become aware of the pleaser's positive contributions by being sensitive to other people. With the integration of sub-personalities, the grace-filled channel becomes unclogged, and we experience release of that which constricts the human spirit. When this occurs, we are in tune with the higher aspect of our selves and those Universal qualities of love, beauty, truth, justice, and wholeness. In more traditional theological language, we are centered in God's will.

A Time for Reflection and Action

Reflect on a time when you felt cut off from life; for example, when you were worried about whether you would be accepted by someone and, hence, you were not able to fully experience the relationship. (+++) Get in touch with these memories and their associated feelings. (+++)

Now reflect on those moments in your life when grace was truly present, when you felt the life giving forces of energy within you; when trust was fully present; when you felt unconditionally accepted. (+++) Reflect on how that facilitated your relationship or experience. (+++) Remember a time when you were fully graceful; when you placed absolute trust in another person or event; when you held nothing back and you allowed yourself to experience the relationship or event in the most beautiful way. (+++)

The choices are ours. Gracefulness invites grace and unconditional acceptance to be present. The presence of grace, the unconditional acceptance of ourselves and of others, is the base upon which the inspirited journey to wholeness can occur.

Chapter 3
CONFESSION

So That's What It Is?

They spaced themselves
On limb and wire
As if to chart
The contour of a melody.
Perhaps they thought
I might capture
The essence of their song by sight.
So limited am I
In hearing beauty
In another's song.
[Carroll Rinehart]

THE HUMANISTIC PSYCHOLOGIST Sidney Jourad, in his Transpersonal Self, cites a classic study by Dr. Bert Goldstein of the concrete behavior of people who were brain-damaged as a result of gunshot wounds received during the First World War. He notes that they displayed a "catastrophic reaction" to any introduction of change in their respective worlds. As long as they experienced no interruptions, and they perceived their world as stable, they could function well. If presented with some new task for which they were not prepared, they would go into a tremendous panic. Jourad makes this observation: "Many people educated in our public school system react to new ideas with outrage or panic as Goldstein's patients did.

Can we regard public education as a functional equivalent to a gunshot wound to the head? Do our socialization practices have effects comparable to brain tumors and arteriosclersis?"(16)

Does Goldstein' observation have any bearing on the unproductive strategies of refusing to acknowledge attitudes or behaviors that are self-limiting in our human encounters as well as in other activities? (+++)

What are the consequences when fear or doubt result in our defensively clinging to outmoded ways of being? (+++) Jourad suggests that there is a clear relationship between self-disclosure and being able to perceive and make sense of the "unremitting disclosure of the world."

Eugene:

I am aware that, to the extent that my preoccupations and fears dominate my actions, I am unavailable to the world. Although seven decades have since passed, I still vividly remember sitting at my assigned desk in a one room country school in western Nebraska, frightened, uninvolved and withdrawn. I was told that I was 'dumb' and I played that role superbly well during most of the first twelve years of my formal education. (It should have been a great learning experience. The dozen or so students in this one room school had an opportunity to hear the recitations of classes either of those students who were ahead or behind them in academic levels.)

I was in so much emotional pain, that for the most part, I withdrew into what seemed like the safety of my own little world. I now recognize that I 'took myself off the hook' in terms of facing up to the learning tasks that I know were easily within my learning abilities. I now know that I allowed myself to be locked into a dumb role. No one else ultimately had the power to put me into that prison.

I vividly remember when, in the middle of the elementary years, I was asked by a teacher to repeat the alphabet. In my panic, I tried to escape the task by suggesting I had learned the alphabet long ago and it was too elementary. I painfully remember the teacher insisting that I complete this recall exercise and still can see the scornful look on her face when half way through the exercise I stumbled badly. During those years, I saw little of the world that was around me. I know that if I had found the courage and the support to be self-disclosing, my memories of those early years would not be so clouded and unreal to me now.

In later college years, I painfully remember how blocked I typically felt. Often I was aware that I had something to contribute to the classroom discussion but was paralyzed by the thought that my attempts to disclose would not be favorably received. Fear not only blocked my sharing, but my reception of the disclosure of others around me who sought to reveal the world as they saw it.

When, with professional colleagues whom I find a bit intimidating, I still find myself blocked in disclosing my thoughts and insights. I all too often hesitate to confess that I either don't understand what it is that they are attempting to disclose, or share the fact that I am not resonating with what they are saying. When I fail to disclose or risk, I am in some way diminished.

Some years ago, I participated in a weekend retreat experience where I felt awkward about the cognitive content that was being shared. If I hadn't liked the facilitators as much as I did, I probably would have had a great deal of resistance to the retreat experience. The participants were seriously invited to get in touch with the energy of the earth by listening to and communicating with the rocks, trees, and animals. The message was that in some way we are a part of the same energy field.

After this particular presentation we were invited to go outside and search for rocks. We were told that we would know when we had found just the right rock. I tried hard to set aside a skeptical attitude. I searched for about thirty minutes. While I did select a rock that I found somewhat attractive, I certainly wasn't aware of any mystical connection.

Once the group had reassembled in our meeting place, we were instructed to lie on the floor and place the rock on our foreheads and enter into a dialogue with our rock. It was suggested that we wait expectantly for some message in this meditative state. There was a long silence without my being aware of anything but my usual internal mental chatter. While I certainly didn't hear an auditory message from the rock, I began to reflect on how long it had been in its present form and tried to imagine the volcanic beginnings that had been instrumental in its creation. I doubt I would have gotten into a rather inspirational kind of meditation if I had not received this assignment.

I confess that I still haven't fully processed the cognitive content of that weekend, but I have been 'haunted' by the experience. In ways that I can not fully understand or explain, the facilitator was an instrument of revelation, revealing the world to me in a way that I had never before seen. My level of awareness regarding inanimate objects as well as other life forms shifted to a new plane. While jogging several days after this retreat, I saw a large bird sitting on a telephone wire. I found myself spontaneously greeting the bird almost as if I were St. Francis of Assissi. How powerful is Jesus' observation that we have eyes to see and yet don't see, ears to hear but do not hear.

Modeling Leadership

A function of an educator is that of a revealer, that is, opening up the world to others. Hence, perhaps the most dynamic quality that a teacher can possess is the ability to confess—by opening oneself, and in a measure the world, to students.

Carroll:

A school was involved in creating and producing an opera. The entire student body had identified the social issues that were to be addressed. Language Arts classes had written the story and transformed the story into a libretto or script. They had written the texts for the arias and choruses. Music classes had composed and orchestrated the music for the tragic tale of an alcoholic.

I remember how powerful it was when one alcoholic teacher chose to be confessional with the students. The teacher had been 'dry' for a year but his memories of his struggle were still much alive. He chose to share his struggles and the daily choices he has to make in his recovery. Of course, it was clearly relevant to problems these students were already experiencing in their lives and was critical information needed to give life to the lead character of the story.

An atmosphere of grace was fully present. The disclosures were honest and freely shared. The story line of the opera was given a new sense of reality. But most important, students began seeking out this teacher to share their struggles, their problems. He modeled in an important way what can happen in a life when one 'owns' what and who one is. New life was breathed into the opera and into the lives of all other people in the school.

Eugene:

When I reflect on the teachers who have had their greatest impact upon me, I realize that much of their influence radiated out from their sense of presence and poise. It was clear that they had a love for learning and were passionate in sharing themselves with their students. They also possessed a self-revealing quality evidenced by their commitment to honesty and integrity. While I have long forgotten most of the cognitive content that they shared, I have not forgotten what Jourard terms their 'inspiriting' quality. In spite of many internal filters that previously both blocked my learning and inhibited an awakening to life, these teachers spoke to me in a way that I gradually began to hear and to see even though that seeing and hearing was often clouded. They made the world begin to come alive. They made it possible for me to take the first tentative and faltering steps toward confessing, both what I didn't know as well as beginning to recognize the truths that had been locked unacknowledged within me.

These key teachers were both gentle and confrontational. In their confrontations, which I perceived as painful, they risked my disorderly and panicked retreat behind barriers that I had carefully but falsely erected to protect me from the potential pain of knowing. From these experiences I have gained a new appreciation of the biblical story of Adam and Eve eating of the fruit of knowledge.

Of course, these teachers were far from perfect. On occasions I faced their wrath that grew out of agendas that had little to do with me. My Greek teacher, who was in her 100th year of life when she passed on, was a member of the faculty of a small, unaccredited, 'fundamentalistic' Bible college. From an academic perspective, it was a school that appeared to have little to offer, particularly in terms of facilities and a credentialed faculty. The learning atmosphere was often heavy with agendas that were oppressive and manipulative. Yet this setting became a crucial bridge for me academically, socially and spiritually. I had not been adequately prepared to enter a usual college or university academic setting. (As an aside, a number of colleagues who were not much better prepared academically or socially than I was eventually ended up with doctoral degrees from major universities.)

At barely seventeen with my 'shaky' academic background, I had little business at that point in my educational awakening being in a Greek class. On one occasion, the instructor, characterized by strict no-nonsense Germanic mannerisms, decided that we were not taking our Greek studies seriously enough. I could tell by the 'set of her jaw' that the test that she announced for the following morning was going to be extraordinarily demanding. My analysis proved to be accurate.

I remember studying from the time I returned from my afternoon job until very late. Following a very short sleep, I arose in the wee hours to continue my preparation for the 'test of fire' that I knew awaited us. I arrived at the classroom exhausted and spent. I remembered having studied with diligence the very tasks on which we were being tested. Yet my foggy, tired mind was unable to reproduce that learning. The harder I tried, the more blocked and immobilized I became. In utter frustration, I finally gave up and became the first to leave the room. The teacher recognized at a glance that I had performed poorly. This apparently confirmed her suspicions that the entire class had been 'coasting.' Before waiting to see my classmates' written responses, she vented her wrath on me and, indirectly, on the rest of the class.

Because of my timidity and the embarrassment of that occasion, I didn't have the courage, until years later, to share with her the energy that I had invested in preparing for that test. My inability to confess my state of exhaustion, which grew out of being spread very thin in an effort to survive financially and academically, resulted in a great deal of personal pain and humiliation. I did what I had often done before. I internalized both my frustrations and unrecognized hurt/anger. Yet this teacher became on of the most significant and influential people to shape my life during that crucial stage of my development. Obviously she saw life through the filters of her own history. Nevertheless, she possessed certain qualities that powerfully influenced me, and several generations of students.

In spite of her 'blind spots' and imperfections, she had a unique ability to call forth talents and hidden gifts that were dormant in students. She encouraged people to confess these possibilities that were waiting to emerge. More often than not, she had a sense of awareness that encouraged her students to be present to the moment. Although the fundamentalistic emotional and social climate of the classrooms was often heavy, she somehow had a way of transcending the barriers and limitations inherent in that environment. I can still hear her spontaneous and contagious laughter that seemed to erupt from her very core. In a system that was rigid and inflexible, she demonstrated a remarkable tolerance for change. Yet she was clearly faithful to the core values of that system.

At a fragile and essentially undisclosing phase in my life, she and others made it possible for me to take halting steps toward openness, openness to my unrecognized potential and also to pain that I tried so hard to deny.

Through the ensuing years I have recognized how vital this setting was for me. Some of the friends that I have valued most over the years shared this learning environment with me.

Bio-physical Implications

From the bio-physical perspective regarding wholeness, the confessional mode has important implications.

Eugene:

I remember hearing Dr. Valerie Hunt, a professor of Human Movement at UCLA, in her lectures state that the source of health is an abundant and resonating interacting energy field. Dis-ease is present to the degree that there is a faulty transaction of energy. She further suggests that the source of all pathology is 'frozen' energy.

She contended that we experience pain because atoms become too dense in the way they are organized in our body at a given point in time. On the other hand, she observed that when we are centered, we can enhance the functioning of the human body. It is not the external forces that ultimately impact energy but is rather our own internal response to these forces.

She also noted that, our thoughts, which are a form of energy, are substantially different when characterized by high versus low energy levels. If Hunt's observations have any degree of validity, it follows that a confessional, disclosing stance can profoundly impact our physical health. Victimization, except for being in the wrong place at the wrong time, is seldom experienced without conceding personal power or energy.

I have often observed, within myself and others, energy blockages experienced in the physical ways of which Hunt speaks. When I was going through a crisis of confidence several years ago, questioning the wisdom of having left an established position to enter private practice in a place where I had few professional contacts, I became aware of a profound restlessness which robbed me of my sleep and peace of mind. I was aware of my lack of centeredness which made it difficult for me to be present to that moment in time.

Even as I write these lines, I'm aware of being uneasy about changing circumstances that could influence my professional life. In such uneasy moments, I find it difficult to be centered as compared to when I am feeling more confident.

I am also aware that a part of me wants to be compliant while another part of me is frightened by this tendency. This fear has proven to be a driven need for change in my life. While I am unable to fully explain this fear, I do know that in taking professional and personal risks, I have often experienced high energy. I suspect that past experiences of high energy that have occurred while taking risks have been reinforced by risk taking behavior.

You Can't Fool Your Body

There is abundant evidence to document the correlation between a troubled spirit and a troubled body. It is also clear that many somatic conditions only marginally respond to the surgeon's knife or to drugs or chemical interventions. This is particularly true of stress-related symptoms. Those in the healing arts can eloquently testify that many persons seek a magical cure for their maladies rather than attempt to deal forthrightly in a confessional way with the factors which more basically contribute to their somatic diseases.

Eugene:

Some years ago I received a request from a physician to see one of his patients who was approaching her thirties. She had had a number of exploratory abdominal surgeries that had resulted in a great deal of scarring. Despite the fact that her surgeons had found no medical complications, her pain did not subside.

A number of sessions of psychotherapy followed with little apparent result. In an effort to have her move past the apparent impasse, I asked her to record her dreams. Initially she indicated that she wasn't having dreams. Then she reported a dream in which she and her mother were crossing a busy street. Her mother was pushing a baby carriage. As they were crossing the street, a car traveling at a high rate of speed unexpectedly crossed the intersection making a left hand turn. Both she and her mother had to scramble to avoid being hit. The baby carriage, however, was struck and the baby killed.

I asked her to assume the role and perspective of the various characters in her dream, one at a time. In the middle of this role playing, in a startled way, she stated that she knew the identity of the baby The baby represented her father. She then shared the story of how her father began to have sexual intercourse with her as she was approaching puberty. This behavior continued regularly until she reached her middle teens when she began to rebel against his sexual overtures.

The meaning of her abdominal pains quickly became clear. No wonder surgery had led nowhere. Her body clearly carried not only the scars of her surgeries but more importantly the scars that reached to the depth of her psyche.

She began to realize that her father had never matured beyond the developmental age of a child and consequently had little or no idea of how to be a father to her. She also began to develop awareness of the anger which had been reflected in her medical symptoms.

This story raises interesting questions for all of us to examine. How have we somatized our spiritual and emotional pain? Or put another way, what are the consequences that we experience when we fail to deal forthrightly with painful events and happenings in our life in less than a confessional way? If we are truly choosing the processes that lead to maturity and wholeness, then confession or "owning what is" is essential.

The High Price of Resentment

While not all of the dimensions are known, there is increasing evidence that there is a significant correlation between resentment and physical distress, particularly with certain types of arthritis. While this correlation needs to be noted, there is not necessarily a one-to-one relationship of arthritis to resentment. Nevertheless it is important to grasp the importance of releasing feelings of hurt and internal pain as a preventative measure. Not to do so is to invite dis-ease.

Think of a time when your physical system reflected a spiritual/ emotional dis-ease. (+++) What kept you from being fully aware and owning the causes of the dis-ease? (+++) What was the graceful moment that made possible the release of the blockage? (+++)

Eugene:

A professor at Michigan State University who left a significant impact on how I see the therapy process was Dr. Bill Kell, now deceased. He was the Director of the University Counseling Center. One of Dr. Kell's physical characteristics was a 'frozen' neck. When he went to look to his right or his left, he had to turn his whole body.

While his lectures clearly had a strong theoretical orientation, they also had a strong experiential flavor. One of his unforgettable stories featured him as a young Army officer stationed overseas confronted by a tragedy of immense proportions that 'knocked the emotional props' from under him. The grief that he experienced was so intense that his whole physical, emotional and spiritual core literally shut down. He was soon bedfast losing his capacity for movement. It seemed apparent that he was literally dying of grief.

He reported that one morning he heard an internal voice inviting him to choose life or death. While this voice did not have a real auditory component, the message was very clear for him. Then and there, he made a commitment to life. In his mind, if he had chosen death, the result of that choice would have been imminent.

While he didn't recover all of the physical mobility that he had before this tragedy, his physical comeback was remarkable. His decision for life led him to choose intellectual pursuits that he would not have otherwise followed. More than that, he developed a remarkable sensitivity as a facilitator of persons who were experiencing blocks in their emotional development.

Another acquaintance from the early fifties made the opposite choice. This woman had broken a hip in a fall some years before we met. That broken hip apparently provided a great deal of hidden benefit that came from holding on to her disabling condition. She refused to walk, even though physically it would not have been a major task to walk again after her injury. She depended upon her neighbors or other volunteers to carry her and her wheel chair up a flight of at least a dozen steps. When she was with a group, she would assume a role of being nearly helpless. Although she was known to maneuver well in her home, she would demand someone to push her wheelchair when in public. Her immobility seemed to be clearly correlated to whether or not other people were present.

She would flatly refuse the offers of assistance to enable her to walk. Even her physician was steadfastly rebuffed in his desire to examine her injured hip. She clearly had chosen a path of isolation and a gradual death.

It is interesting to speculate about why one person chooses life while another chooses a form of lingering lifelessness. Perhaps the latter person is indirectly expressing anger toward the self or toward some significant other. Or the choice may be a desperate yet manipulative plea for love. Perhaps it involves a death wish. It may represent a limited repertoire of strategies from which a choice is being made.

Actually we make daily choices between the qualities that lead to life or those that eventually lead to physical, emotional and/or spiritual death. The Old Testament prophet Joshua exhorts his people to choose life or to choose death, adding that he was coming down on the side of life.

More About Choices

The processes of grace are always linked to the processes of life. The moment we choose death, the dynamic movement of grace has been thwarted.

Eugene:

A number of years ago, a client with whom I been working, announced that she was suicidal. She had known intense despair for a number of years. Long periods of hospitalization and excessive shock treatments had not been able to dispel her despair.

Options were offered to her, including another hospitalization. She refused them all, noting that she planned to drive into a tree at 100 miles an hour when she left my office.

While there is typically a strong element of manipulation in suicidal threats, mental health professionals and medical personnel usually swing into action when a serious threat of suicide is heard. My response surprised even me. I told her that I would honor her decision even though I opted for life. I further stated that if she carried out this threat I would attempt to communicate to her pre-teen son, daughter, and husband that her choice of death was her attempt to resolve her pain.

The next week she returned to my office with bottles of medication that she had managed to accumulate stating that she wanted to commit suicide in my office. Again my response to her was that I still honored her choice, but would not assist her in implementing her choice because I could only assist in reaching goals that were consistent with my ethical values.

Admittedly, I would have gladly referred her elsewhere, but within our system I was the last person in the chain. When I later announced to her that I was moving to Arizona she stated that she was in love with me. My response was to express delight in her expression of love. I added that love originates from God. I made it clear that our love would not be expressed in sexual ways but deeply caring ways, as a brother and sister might show their mutual affection. She was enormously relieved. In fact, it was the beginning of real movement toward her healing. In earlier sessions, she had confessed that she had had a sexual experience with the pastor of the church she attended. Interestingly, she reported that this pastor had condemned adultery in rather harsh terms from the pulpit. Understandably, from her negative perspective, she had twisted his message to mean that she had been the temptress while he was the innocent victim.

The last I heard about her was that she was enrolled in a community college and was, for the most part, depression free. She had clearly started down a path that leads to life. Strong elements that promoted her healing included her confession of 'inner secrets' and my acceptance of her feelings of love for me. It was important also to frame this message of love in a way that had new and healing meaning for her.

What are the Risks?

When there is a heart-felt confession involving significant risk there is a real chance that the life giving process will be activated. It may be akin to the immune process which blocked, in the cancer victim, suddenly is reactivated with healing results. The question of why one would choose to hold on to pain that is expressed in both somatic and psycho-spiritual ways, when releasing it is clearly an option, has no easy answers. All of us are aware at some level of 'hanging onto,' harboring, or perversely cherishing a carefully nurtured resentment, hurt or fear. Why is it so difficult to let resentments die, hurts abate, and fears vanish?

Many of us remember reading about Japanese soldiers staying hidden in caves for thirty years following World War II. They remained prisoners through their isolation—isolation which in fact was totally unnecessary. Think of all they missed in terms of being with family and friends, not to mention scientific and technological development.

A young Associate Pastor of a congregation was doing his first funeral service for a person with whom he had become well-acquainted. The deceased, a young man, had died as a result of a tragic automobile accident caused by another person who was under the influence of alcohol. Suffering severe head injuries, he had clung to life for several weeks and then, mercifully, died.

The young minister read the scriptures with the poise of an experienced minister. But when he began to share some of the ways that the deceased had impacted him, he broke into uncontrolled sobbing. All who had gathered to mourn and celebrate the life of this young man wept with the pastor. It was a time of 'letting go,' which launched a time of healing.

While our internal defenses, carefully accumulated and preserved across time, are functional if appropriately used, more often than not they represent overkill. Most of the fears we harbor and the resentments we nourish do not merit the investment that we make in them.

Eugene:

Several years ago a group of about thirty people gathered for a potluck which was to be followed by a Lenten study group. The evening's discussion was to be on poverty.

As we gathered, I somewhat reluctantly met a street person who had drifted in to share the meal with us. Obviously he had not bathed for several days, perhaps weeks. His appearance left a great deal to be desired. I passively avoided contact with him while I ate. Following the meal, I noticed that he was sitting alone, waiting for the group discussion to begin.

Feeling that someone should speak to him, I tentatively engaged him in conversation without much enthusiasm. I learned that he had been sleeping under the bridge at night since his arrival in Tucson.

I also learned that at one point in his life he had briefly attended college, and had been involved in the drug culture. While I knew him somewhat better by the time that the group discussion began, I still was not very involved or very concerned about him.

The group leader introduced a short film about a Greek Orthodox priest whom he had met in a Middle Eastern country. He spoke about the paradox of having nothing but, at the same time, having everything. As the discussion progressed, I was struck by the irony of the discussion. All of us, except one uninvited guest, were going to be sleeping in comfortable beds that night while he would be sleeping under a bridge. I became aware of my discomfort at having a 'smelly drifter' in our midst while we casually talked about poverty. My heart was pounding. I was troubled. Did I really want to confront our esteemed leader? Did I truthfully want to be up front about the issue involving this real live person among us who was poverty stricken?

I was aware that my voice sounded strained as I suggested to the group that we should turn to the stranger in our midst if we really wanted to learn about poverty. I soon realized that I had placed the stranger in an awkward position. Somewhat reluctantly the group began to struggle with this person's presence among us. A person from one of the city agencies volunteered to get him a room for the night at a hotel which contracts to provide for such persons on a one or two night basis. This action had responded to a need but had missed the larger point. The way our group skirted the issue of poverty that evening didn't seem very graceful. We really hadn't availed ourselves of the opportunity to have a full encounter with the stranger. Wse didn't actually take him in.

For weeks I was unable to shake him from my thoughts. While this brief experience with him felt unfinished, I realized in a small way he had been my teacher. Perhaps he had been an angel that came to us for the most part unrecognized. Although we did not allow the potential for gracefulness to be fully realized, none the less he had provided us with an opportunity for significant self-confrontation.

I'm not at all sure that others present during that evening experienced the moment as powerfully as I. All I know is that I was haunted (creatively, I hope) by the experience. It wouldn't let me go.

As I continued to struggle with this episode, a part of me wondered whether I was reading something into the story that wasn't there. Was this part of me so concerned about approval and consensus that I couldn't see the learning as authentic or valid unless, or until, this kind of concurrence took place? Is it possible that this unexpected teacher touched something deep within me that was poverty stricken, unacceptable, unkempt, offensive? It is possible that I was brought face to face with something I would rather not have seen. If so, was Christ's proclamation of our 'not having been present to the least of these' confronting me? Christ also said that the meek and lowly are fortunate for the whole wide world belongs to them. Did Christ's observations apply to me in the situation just described at a level I was just beginning to see?

I feel certain that this 'drifter' had no idea that he had been my teacher, that I had had a glimpse of a stranger in me as a result of our chance encounter. He had been a channel for grace. In some respects, I felt I had met the Christ in a startling and totally unexpected way.

I didn't try to share with our group that this unexpected encounter had touched me in a rather profound way. Nor did I attempt to share with them. Primarily because of my strong approval needs I tend to distrust experiences which do not result in external affirmation. Something, however, wouldn't allow me to discount the value of this encounter.

As I now reflect on this experience, two decades after this event, I wonder what response would have been appropriate. I certainly was sensitive to the 'drifter' in our presence and would not have wanted to put him on the spot again. Yet my response to the superficial reaction of the group troubles me. What kept me from confronting the leader about the fact that we didn't truly receive the stranger in our midst when the essence of meeting was to deal with the issue of 'having nothing but at the time having everything?' While the stranger certainly could have used a warm motel to shower and get a good night's sleep, that wasn't his most pressing need. Was my need for affirmation so intense that I wasn't willing to 'go to the wall' as far as our group's facing up to its basic responsibilities as people of faith? In my judgment, we missed an opportunity to be the Good Samaritan and provide a place where healing could occur. I missed the opportunity to represent what I believe to be at the core of our reason for being.

Family histories are filled with very minor problems that are unowned, unconfessed and unreleased. Such problems can escalate into major dysfunctions and destroy harmony and integrity. The graceful thing to do, in the very beginning, is to own what is felt and experienced, then to openly disclose those feelings and move to what is truly important.

A valid confession, by its very nature, requires giving up emotional bomb shelters that have consciously or unconsciously designed to protect against some real or imagined painful feelings.

Taking the Next Step

Eric Fromm, the German psychiatrist-philosopher, in his book *To Have Or To Be* devotes many pages to the "having mode" and the "being mode" of existence." In the having mode, there is no alive relationship between me and what I have. It and I have become things, and I have it, because I have the force to make it mine. But there is also a reverse relationship. It has me, because my identity, i.e. of sanity, rests upon my having it (and as many things as possible). The having mode of existence is not established by an alive, productive process between subject and object; it makes things of both object and subject. The relationship is one of deadness, not aliveness."(17)

Maintaining resentment is the refusal to surrender the power of a toxic attitude that one person holds in relationship to another. Ironically, as such defensive patterns (which often resemble arsenals) accumulate, the person seeking to maintain security through accumulation ends up not being self-protective but, in some measure, self-destructive. A failure to confess then bears a strong relationship to this having mode of existence; a failure that leads to pathology of both body and spirit. The being mode, which is dynamic and alive, bears a strong relationship to the "inspiriting" qualities of confession. All of us feel this pull between inspiriting qualities and the need for security—between risking and "playing it safe."

Eugene:

There was an experience during the years of graduate school that changed how I perceived the process of confession. It involved a young mother who was struggling with the depths of depression. In the midst of despair, she took great risks in the therapy hour that not only impacted on her life but on mine as well. She had grown up in a committed Christian home where both the political and religious values were solidly conservative. Her father was, in many respects, seen as the conscience of his small rural township and county. He was the first to champion important altruistic causes and clearly a person who was highly respected, even by those who disagreed with his politics.

As a high school student, this young lady had been very attractive. Any young man would have considered himself lucky to claim her as a 'steady.' In many respects she had incorporated all of the values of her parents. One young man, popular primarily because of his athletic abilities in high school, was drawn to her. Though she sensed a disparity in the values she and this young man held, her female peers told her how lucky she was to have 'snared' his interest. Not trusting her own internal guidance system, she formed a relationship with him.

Her values about sex before marriage mirrored those of her parents. He, like many of his peers, saw being the aggressor as the appropriate 'macho' thing to do. For a long time, she resisted his moves. Then on one occasion her resistance crumbled. She became pregnant.

She managed to hide the pregnancy from her parents for nearly eight months. Even though she tried to pretend that 'it wasn't so,' she was inundated with feelings of guilt, fear and shame. When the 'truth came out' her well-meaning parents tried to 'do the right thing.' They took this young couple across the state border for a marriage ceremony the very weekend they became aware of her pregnancy. It was seen as the discrete thing to do.

However, their marriage was in trouble from the very beginning. Additional children quickly followed the birth of the first child. This couple had little meaningful communication and their sexual contacts were loaded with all the earlier guilt and pain of her first lonely pregnancy. She experienced intense despair. Suicide was considered an unforgivable sin and she found herself pushing back suicidal thoughts. To avoid the chaos of her life, she would have gladly committed herself to a long term psychiatric institution.

In the midst of her despair, another person gave her the sensitive attention for which she had longed. She responded like a drowning person clinging to everything or everyone that is available. While this relationship did not become a sexual one, it possessed a kind of intimacy which she found healing. She acknowledged that, on one hand, her behavior had been inappropriate and she felt guilty. On another level she felt loved. In this relationship she had experienced a measure of grace and healing.

Her powerful sharing with him, and later with me in the therapy room, was clearly healing to her. Her experience forever challenged my previous perception of the gift of grace. I became aware, in a way that I had never before realized, that when love is present in any degree, to that degree God is present. In such insightful moments, grace comes to meet us in unexpected ways, and in unexpected places.

A Time for Reflection and Action

Reflect on a time when you felt blocked from fully experiencing a relationship and/or from fully participating in an event. (+++) Remember the feelings and impressions you had at the time. Note any fears you may have held. (+++). Did you fully acknowledge and own the blocks? (+++) Did you choose to talk through the problem, to clarify the blocks, with a person you fully trusted? (+++) Think through that experience again. How might you have approached it differently? How might you have owned all the feelings and thoughts associated with it? Imagine that you have the ability to play the whole experience again, changing the transactions for more positive results. How would you do differently? (+++)

Choose an area of your life in which you feel blocked (intellectually, spiritually, socially, physically or emotionally), and write down all you know about that blockage. (+++) If you have fears, list them that you might more fully own them. (+++) Decide how such responses once served you. Determine how they help or hinder you now. (+++) When you have worked through the ownership more fully, move to the next chapter dealing with repentance.

Chapter 4
REPENTANCE

So What Do You Want to Do?

Through endless
Time
Man processes,
Works and finds
Sublime
Fulfillment,
Tranquility
In his love for all
Mankind.

So
Short
The span
That's given
Man.
So long becomes his quest.

Grant him assurance;
Affirm him that he may know.
Give him vision that he may see

The path
He's taken
Is linked
To
Eternity.
[Carroll Rinehart]

REPENTANCE IS AN important step in a sequential process leading to wholeness. It must be preceded by confession. Repentance is the beginning step in changing priorities and, hence, in changing behavior in creative ways.

Eugene:

An intellectually gifted male in his late 40s was in psychotherapy. He had been an alcohol abuser but had managed to quit drinking without the help of any social network such as AA. However, the tools he had successfully used in changing his drinking behavior simply didn't work when he tried to stop smoking.

He reported that in his middle elementary school years he began to smoke regularly. When he reached his middle school years, he was smoking heavily. By the time he reached his adult years, he was smoking three or four packs of unfiltered camel cigarettes.

At the point he decided to seek therapy he had developed a serious case of asthma and emphysema. X-rays revealed menacing spots appearing on his lungs. Still he smoked in spite of his announced intention to quit.

With the knowledge that he was a highly visual person, he was invited to picture that part of himself (sub-personality) that was intent on smoking, gravely influencing the state of his health. He was also invited to create a dialogue with that sub-personality, seeking to understand its agenda.

The resulting dialogue clearly indicated that one aspect of himself was angry and frustrated. The target of those feelings, which he committed to writing, focused initially on an unsatisfying sexual relationship with his wife. From the perspective of that sub-personality, death was seen as an acceptable way of leaving the relationship. After several similar visualization sessions, accompanied by spontaneous internal dialogue, this sub-personality, which had insisted on holding on to the smoking behavior, began to take on quite a different role. It became a member of the Board of Directors of his internal organization.

Dialogue with this Board Member over several weeks of therapy led this sub-personality to make a decision to resign from the Board. The statement contained in the letter of resignation went something like this: 'When our organization was still young, I had a useful role to play. Smoking seemed like the thing to do. It was a way of trying to gain status and assert a measure of independence. As the company grew in size and complexity, I began to sense that the function of smoking didn't do what it once seemed to do. In fact, I began to feel a measure of irrelevance as well as inadequacy, particularly as my peers no longer placed priority on smoking. Actually it had become the thing not to do. I now realize I have not geared up for the demands that now face this complex organization. I feel it is in the best interest of the organization that I resign my position on The Board.' As he read this letter, tears streamed down his cheeks, it was clear that his smoking days were numbered.

One common theological definition of repentance is to change directions. What is needed is to create behaviors that will still meet the intention of an old undesirable behavior without 'staying stuck' in that behavior when it is no longer appropriate. It is somewhat analogous to a two-year-old child who learns to ride a tricycle. Although the child's new skills are indeed important age-related achievements, if this person is still using the same tricycle riding skills at age twenty-two, something has seriously gone wrong in the maturational process. Even though a new behavior may be weak and tenuous in the beginning, it is an important building block in the developmental process. Gradually it strengthens and the old gives way to the new. Life grows on!

The failure to repent reflects a breakdown in the gradual development process, a failure to take the next step. The client above, stuck in smoking behavior, represented a flaw in that process.

Eugene:

I was teaching a graduate holistic health course at one of the highly respected state universities in the deep South. On the first day of class, I outlined the requirements of the course and then announced that the students would have the opportunity to select their own course grades and conduct their own assessments. One standard guideline for this assessment was the requirement that each student meet with me and demonstrate how his/her participation in the course had resulted in significant changes in thinking and behaving.

One of the students was a former medical student with a history of chronic indecisiveness. In his third year, he discovered he had a brain tumor. Surgery, performed by one of his respected professors, proved the tumor to be benign.

However, following the surgery he experienced grand mal seizures and was unable to finish medical school. While the student was still gaining consciousness in the recovery room, his surgeon gently attempted to assure him that all was well. With soft, soothing statements that the student was safe and had nothing to worry about, the surgeon added that he could just relax and rest comfortably. He reassured the student that he didn't need to make any decisions.

Unfortunately the surgeon's well-intentioned, trance-like statements had inadvertently reinforced the student's underdeveloped decision making ability. As a result, following his recovery, his indecisive behavior became nearly incapacitating.

When it came time for the student to meet with me and make a decision about his grade for the academic course, he was terrified. I was convinced that he had indeed put great effort into the class. He could articulate well the ways that he had accumulated new understanding and skill in this area. When I asked him to make a decision about his grade based on his growth and development, he began to stutter and insist that I make the decision. I reminded him that at the beginning of the course students had been informed they would be required to make their own assessments about their grade-assessments that would be honored unless I suspected the student had been fraudulent in this assessment process.

He then announced that he was about to experience a grand mal seizure. He handed me instructions that he carried in his shirt pocket about how a helping person should react. I commented that his body had a long history of seizures and knew how to respond. I asked him to look around the room to see if there were changes that needed to be made for his safety and comfort. After a quick assessment, he stated the room was satisfactory. I then asked him to lie down and give his body permission to have a seizure.

His seizure lasted a number of minutes. Although not an expert on seizures, I sensed he was not in peril—that the seizure would follow the usual pattern. While keeping an eye on him, I reviewed the course papers he had written. (I confess that I was very thankful that a colleague or a student hadn't knocked on my door during this episode.)

Following the seizure, he was not fully conscious for another ten minutes or so. When he began to think more clearly, I asked him if he had yet decided on a grade for the course. He gave me a look that can only be described as utter astonishment. After a moment of silence, he responded that he would take a grade of B. I assured him that he would receive his requested semester grade.

The next day he called me to state that he really thought he deserved an A for the course; a grade I awarded him after he made his request. While I didn't have contact with him after the term ended, I suspect that he learned something about his seizures that he hadn't consciously known before.

Was he able to let go of previous behavior that had been limiting to him? I suspect that he did. If so, this kind of repentance could have been a liberating moment for him.

A Price to Pay

It is not surprising there are dire consequences when the experience of repentance does not take place. The cleansing process is blocked. Throughout history, wars have fomented when this cleansing has notoccurred. Entire cultural groups have been known to build on animosities that have been perpetuated for centuries. Recent conflicts in the Middle East, in Eastern Europe, and many other places give eloquent testimony to the importance of moving beyond the old barriers that both divide and debilitate the human spirit.

If we take seriously the proposition that, as individuals, we are the world in microcosm, then it becomes crucial that repentance begin within each of us and radiate outward like the waves that result from the pebble being dropped in a lake, waves that move out in ever-widening circles.

Carroll:

One Sunday I was invited to present the sermon in my church. I prepared to make it as helpful as possible to the needs of the people. In that attempt I not only included scriptural references to my central theme but also psychological references.

Following the service many members of the congregation stopped to express their appreciations. All, that is, but one person who only said, in a rather stern tone, 'It was too psychological.' That single critique devastated me. For some time thereafter I refused other invitations to speak before groups.

What created such a block? Was it my 'pleaser' sub-personality? Was it my 'critical judge?'

What kept me from accepting his response with a simply 'thank you,' for I had truly attempted to make psychological awareness a part of my shared thoughts?

For months I withdrew from activities. I even considered leaving the group. Then the person who had been my external critic left. While reconciliation between that person and me has not occurred, I am aware that a resolution has occurred within me.

How did it happen? While I am aware that I have unfinished business with that external judge, I am also aware that we probably have little opportunity to heal the divisions between us. In the first place, he probably did not know what was going on within me, so effective am I in hiding my hurt! Moreover, we have no common setting to work on a relationship. Hence the relationship remains fractured.

It was important for me to achieve integration within myself. This

I did by talking with friends. That step provided a place of grace within me. Second, it was also important to publicly own, before others, what had gone on within me. I chose to do that in the context of another sermon in church, delivered to those I care about.

Consistent with the hypothesis of this book, that there is a sequential relationship between confession, repentance, forgiveness and reconciliation, I realized that owning my feelings (confession) would not be possible without the desire for change (repentance). My actions leading to repentance, or choosing a new direction for my action, required that I complete the prior step of confession.

Being fully repentant facilitates forgiveness. Before I could integrate the intentions of the sub-personality that had been so devastated by this experience, it was necessary to confess that this sub-personality, my own critical judge, had taken over my Center before the process of forgiveness could be internalized. Once I forgave myself, the process of reconciliation occurred within me. I was once more whole. Should my external judge and I ever meet again, I can be fully present to myself and him. External reconciliation is dependent upon and must be congruent with internal reconciliation.

Eugene:

I remember a man who was the only child of a farm couple who lived successful but modest lives. In spite of having a large farm with excellent soil, the man's parents lived with the distorted belief that they were poor, that life was threatening and that the world was an unsafe place. Well-intentioned, cautious people, they would never knowingly harm a soul.

They kept a tight rein on their son's life. When he married, as expected by his parents, he and his new bride lived on the home place in an upstairs apartment. To them, their daughter-in-law, who resented being under their control, was ungrateful. As the situation became increasingly intolerable to the daughter-in- law, she chose to leave the homestead after the birth of a daughter.

Not realizing that their behavior had played an instrumental role in her decision to leave, her in-laws felt confused and deeply hurt.

Following the breach in the family, I doubt the parents questioned or re-examined their world view and the way they formed relationships.

Their son, who had never left home, subsequently developed severe arthritis In many respects, his disease was a symbol for the many ways he had become immobilized in his life.

I remember dropping in for an unannounced, informal visit. I expected the son and his father would be in the barn. As I approached, I saw they were trying to guide a frightened young calf into a pen. Not wanting to disturb their effort, I observed without announcing my presence. The father, then about seventy years of age, was yelling at his fifty-year-old son because the son had, inadvertently, allowed the calf to get by him. The son's restricted mobility from his arthritic condition had kept him from moving quickly enough to thwart the calf's escape.

The father's words still ring painfully in my ears: 'What's the matter with you. Don't you have any sense?'

Basically a good person with a limited view of the world, the father saw little need for repentance on his part. The flaw, inadequacy, ineptitude was always in the other person from his limited world view. Why, one might ask, did these parents hold such a death grip on their own lives and the life of their only begotten son. We do not know all the factors that caused them to respond as they did. We can only surmise about the hurts and struggles causing their values to be shaped as they were. They were living out patterns set in their lives as they grew, and were undoubtedly influenced by their parents and grandparents.

It is often difficult for us to be fully cognizant of the factors that shape our behavior. It is important, however, that we know ourselves and that we use our awareness to help us let go of behaviors that no longer serve us. In his book, *7 Habits of Highly Effective People*, Stephen Covey, a leadership facilitator living in Utah, includes, as a general theme, the need to fully understand the needs and intentions of our sub-personalities through the use of meditation and visualization.

Why Is It So Tough To Let Go?

At the heart of the processes that we are calling graceful is the need to 'let go.' It has been hypothesized that one of the reasons we cling to old behavior is our deeply rooted instinctual fear of dying. People with an acute psychiatric diagnosis often display an inordinate fear of death. It is our contention that, to the extent a person integrates the process of healing, to that degree one loses the fears that are associated with physical death.

In the case of the parents discussed above, 'playing it safe' became more associated with the forces of death than the forces of life. No wonder Jesus stated it was fundamental that in order to be fully alive one had to move beyond the fear of death.

Rollo May, in his book *Courage to Create*, discusses the nature of creativity in human encounters. (18)

He describes a talented professional with whom he worked in psychoanalysis. This young man would suddenly get an idea for an excellent story and would develop a full outline in his mind which could have been written up without much additional effort. However, he was reluctant to take the step of committing his ideas to paper. In extended sessions with this young man, May discovered that he had a need to show what a gifted person he was. Apparently this need was satisfied through his elaboration of lofty and 'heady' story plots. May concluded this student was stymied in bringing his creative ideas to fruition because he remained in a state of "being almost ready to create." He blocked when it came time to take the next step of committing himself to the discipline of writing.

A Time to Reflect

What keeps us from the repentance process? (+++) What in our fear of being misunderstood and/or vulnerable contributes to this kind of blockage? (+++) In releasing some of 'the stuff' that keeps us from taking the next step, we risk the possibility of losing our defenses that we have relied on—defenses that are likely dysfunctional. What might you be risking? (+++)

Moving In The Right Direction

The education system has often eliminated activities and programs that help individuals become more whole. The result can be an excessive concentration on what doesn't work. For example, to eliminate the arts, in order to concentrate on improving test scores or meet restrictive budgets, denies learners access to other ways of learning and knowing that promote the opportunity to become more whole.

Eugene:

A creative master-teacher of Neurolinguistic Programming made a statement in a seminar that I have never forgotten. Speaking to the audience of psychotherapists he said, if what you're doing with a particular client isn't working, do anything different. He further commented that therapists, when working with difficult situations involving their clients, often persist in trying harder to do what isn't working—typically with counter-productive results. I suspect that observation doesn't apply solely to therapists.

Marriages that are in need of wholeness and opportunities to become playful and creative often embrace and settle for patterns that are counter-productive. Churches also fail to recognize that habitual forms and practices can thwart the release of a celebrative spirit, a failure that prevents their renewal. How often persons in a job becomes stuck and stale because they are afraid of stepping out of established boundaries. Consequently, they fail to be energized and find joy in their work.

I vividly remember a time when six or seven colleagues and I were involved in advanced hypnosis training. We had pooled our funds and arranged for one of the top teachers in the country to spend time with us. When we got to that part of the training where we were working one-on-one, I was paired with a former Associate Dean of the Medical School at the University of Arizona. His credentials were impressive. Not only was he an M.D. and Ph.D., but he was also trained as a Shakespearean actor. Moreover, he had an awesome physical presence. To say that I was a bit intimidated by the match is a gross understatement.

In the role-playing task, he was instructed to be an angry client who had consulted with me for a long time without benefit. According to this scenario, he had paid many dollars for ineffective services. I, on the other hand, was given the task of establishing rapport with him. However, I was restricted to the use of just two words in response to his angry statements, 'That's right.' I could use any tone of voice or any kind of body language that I wanted but only accompanied with those two words.

My doctor-actor friend quickly got into his role. Everything I tried only caused his anger to build. At first he was acting but soon he was responding with genuine anger to my limited response of, 'that's right.'

The trainer, watching from the sideline, observed that I was getting more immobilized by the minute. Finally he came over and whispered in my ear, out of earshot of the person with whom I was interacting, 'You've forgotten to breathe,' having observed my 'paralysis.' I quickly recognized that I had, indeed, been restricting my breathing and, hence, was limiting my intake of oxygen. The result was a buildup of carbon dioxide in my brain that was clouding my responses. I began 'gasping' for air, trying to change the pattern of my involvement in the situation. Nothing, however, worked. I was only digging myself into a deeper hole.

Finally the trainer returned and this time whispered the instruction to see my partner as a six-year-old boy throwing a temper tantrum. I was able to quickly develop that imagery. Suddenly this impressive six foot-plus dashing, competent professional became a tantrum-throwing six-year-old boy.

My verbal utterances were still limited to the two words, 'that's right,' but something within me changed. I became poised and the threat that I had experienced, earlier, vanished. My role-playing partner later inquired what the trainer had told me. He noted that, after the instructor whispered in my ear the second time, he had been unable to maintain the level of anger that had been building in him. The change that occurred essentially within me had evoked a desirable change in him as well.

If feeling anxious and threatened are, indeed, major forces in keeping us immobilized, are such feelings essentially a function of external sources or are they a result of internal perceptions? Why is it that what one person sees as a threat is may not be threatening to another? (+++)

The following story, likely mythical, makes this point in a telling way. It is the story of twin brothers whose immigrant parents died shortly after the brothers became adults. Neither married. The one brother was a free spirited person who never took life very seriously. In the days when "hobos" traveled on top of railroad boxcars, he went wherever a particular train happened to go. His pattern, after several months of riding the rails, was to return to his small hometown near a metropolitan center where his twin had become very wealthy. Embarrassed by his penniless brother who periodically dropped into town, the wealthy brother typically had given his "hobo" brother money to leave. This drama was repeated over a number of years.

As a result of a stock market crash, the wealthy brother lost most of his millions. Barely managing to salvage $100,000, he became so stressed and anxious that he had a fatal heart attack. His sole heir was the wandering brother whom no one knew how to locate.

After the passage of several months, the surviving brother returned to his hometown. When he was told that his deceased twin had left him an inheritance of one hundred thousand dollars, he was so shocked by the unbelievable news that he also had a heart attack and died.

Clearly this story emphasizes that each man perceived reality in his own unique and limited way. Neither of them could let go of his respective beliefs. Ultimately their beliefs led to their deaths.

Repentance requires a willingness to let go of dysfunctional, non-reality-based old patterns to embrace a new way of being.

Eugene:

One of the most difficult confessional moments for me came at my parents' fiftieth wedding anniversary. I had been asked to give the sermon on this occasion. While I cared for my parents, I really didn't know them well. I had left home without their permission or blessing at the age of sixteen. However they did not attempt to block my moving a thousand miles away.

In the years following my departure, I had made short visits about once every three years. Exposure to a much broader environment than I had known in rural western Nebraska had a considerable impact on my world view. Particularly significant had been the years that I had spent in the military as well as in a university setting.

My initial thoughts about giving a sermon on this special anniversary were about offering some complimentary platitudes, whether fitting or not. However, I became increasingly uncomfortable with such an approach. In consultation with valued friends, especially Carroll, I reached the conclusion that a significant element would be missing from the festive celebrative moments if I didn't make a serious attempt to be confessional. I decided to trace our history from Friesland through Russia to the family's immigration to the United States. Since there had been a great deal of drama in this history, some participants had been left with emotional scars. I noted some of the pain and the courage experienced by my parents both before and during their married years. Included were memories related to the Great Depression and the long periods of drought, accompanied by dust storms, that purportedly encircled the earth for three years before the atmosphere was cleansed.

I also attempted to describe my admiration of my father's decision to become a clergyman, while also continuing to be a farmer just as I was entering into high school. While both his education and opportunities for service were limited, he had met his responsibilities to his family and congregation with conviction in the face of great obstacles.

I went on to describe some of the emotional obstacles he had known as a result of his family's isolation from its Mennonite roots. My paternal grandfather had in effect been shunned by the religious community because he violated some rules of the church that would now be seen as laughable. As a result, my father and his siblings were not well received either in the Mennonite community or by the larger community that looked at Mennonites with considerable suspicion.

Since my father's father had not chosen to be a farmer, mine had not developed strong farming skills. In addition, he had been further isolated through his marriage. My mother had come from a strong Mennonite family who disapproved of my father's family. Hence their marriage did not receive her family's blessing even though my mother's father did eventually give them a quarter section of land to farm. In an attempt to gain acceptance and approval by my mother's family, my father did what he thought was expected of a good farmer. Beyond that there were few work options available to him.

I remain convinced their eventual switch to a fundamentalist church after years of isolation and peripheral religious involvement was prompted in large part by the acceptance that this group provided for them. However, this switch apparently isolated them even further from their Mennonite roots.

Faced with low esteem and little community support from their Mennonite community, they did not have the opportunity to learn effective parenting skills. My father's approach to discipline was to demand total obedience. If he interpreted a look that suggested any form of defiance, it was cause for a severe 'whipping.' My father had little understanding that the rage he felt when administering this punishment was somehow related to the rage that had been building in his own psyche for a long period of time.

In that sermon I acknowledged that we were both benefactors, as well as victims, of our history. I also confessed that, as a young parent, I too had used physical discipline as a way of dealing with my internal rage when dealing with my children. Quoting the biblical passage that all had sinned and come short of the glory of God, I announced that it was time for all of us to experience forgiveness and move on to the celebration of this beautiful fiftieth anniversary event.

While this confessional statement was distressing to my father, whose theology held that a converted person lived above sin, it was liberating for me. Even though I had cared for my parents, for years I had had difficulty being in their presence for any period of time. I tended to attribute this barrier to the fact that we had many different life experiences that had shaped our perceptions and there was little common ground to share. I began to realize I had managed to store the hurts of childhood in such a secret inner place, that my childhood seemed almost a vacant blur. I also recognized that my attempts to deal with this emotional and spiritual pain had been ineffective.

Before this event, I had had difficulty contacting them, either by letter or telephone. Subsequently, I found I could visit without the overwhelming sense of restlessness I had experienced earlier. While the setting and circumstances of my visits really hadn't changed, I had changed. I could enter into their world with considerable ease. It was at that time I established the practice of calling them weekly.

I look back to that fiftieth wedding anniversary celebration many years ago, grateful that I took the risk of being confessional and launched the first steps toward repentance. That memory is still a powerful one for me. What was the enabling event that gave me permission to take the approach that confession was needed before a true time of celebration could be experienced? The moment when I knew that I could do no other, to use a phrase from Martin Luther, came out of my discussion with Carroll. I doubt if I would have reached that conclusion by myself. It was truly an affirming moment when I knew that the risk had to be taken regardless of how my siblings, parents, other family members or friends might view my disclosure. Incidentally, my siblings were quite uncertain about the appropriateness of my remarks for this special occasion.

The preparation for the event was exhausting. I re-worked my comments many times to assure myself that I made my best effort to avoid being judgmental while being openly confessional. My confession had to include the blocks that I had experienced with my parents and how we both had contributed to them.

I felt sad that my father interpreted my remarks as a personal criticism toward him rather than an attempt to be confessional. A long chain of events begun generations ago had resulted in brokenness that had been acted out in all of our lives. I also regretted that he experienced some depression as he re-played the tape-recorded remarks that I had made.

While some internal dialogue did occur between my 'pleaser' and my critical 'judge,' this dialogue was rather quickly resolved. The much larger internal response was a sense of liberation. For decades I had played a role in the presence of my parents. I suddenly understood why I felt so uncomfortable in their presence. I hadn't wanted to confront or upset them, and had rationalized that there was little point in upsetting them since our contacts were so limited.

However, my overall response was one of relief. All of the avoidance that had built up over the years was now gone. I felt for the first time that I had gained a set of parents. I could appreciate them now for who they were rather than judge them for what they had or had not done.

As I reflected on what contributed to this powerful healing moment for me, I have noted the central importance of feeling safe to work through both the emotional and cognitive issues that were involved in developing the themes presented at the anniversary celebration. Carroll was there to challenge the places where I got off track as well as confront me where I wasn't dealing up front with issues that were a part of my personal and family history. In short, he was immensely facilitative in helping me develop a process that would lead to healing.

My parents both passed away just weeks before their seventieth wedding anniversary. They died just seven weeks apart. I was surprised and honored that they had asked that I give the sermon at their memorial service. The service was held in the Mennonite Church in the presence of the very people from whom they had initially experienced isolation. It was a time of celebrating their life and faith and honoring their memory. The final healing had occurred.

When Blockages Occur

When the processes of grace are blocked, when we do not confess and deal forthrightly with such blockage, when we do not seek repentance and experience forgiveness and reconciliation, a deterioration of the life-forces occurs that robs us of spiritual awareness. As a result of this deterioration, we no longer perceive and respond to the forces of life around us. A kind of deadness sets in and a cancer of the spirit begins to eat away at the fabric of our lives.

Have you experienced moments of blockage which kept you from being fully aware of and owning the causes of any dis-ease? (+++) Was there a graceful moment that made possible the release of such blockage? (+++).

From the perspective of Psychosynthesis, the integration of mind/body/emotion is critical to the experience of wholeness. In some respects the mind/body/emotion aspects of our being are similar to sub-personalities in that they are representations of who we appear to be. Yet we are far more than is expressed or experienced through our mind, our body and our emotions. Previously we described dis-identification. Assagioli spoke of the importance of dis-identification and of gaining a significant measure of internal objectivity by using that process.

Implicit in this radically different strategy of assessing ourselves and others is the notion that the core of one's being, one's real self (the Center) can be accessed through the process of reflection and meditation. According to Assagioli, the Center is the source of wisdom. From the Center we can communicate with the mind/ body/emotion through the imaginative visual process. Assagioli also says that we can access the sub-personalities in much the same way.

We Ain't There Yet!

In his book *Sacred Eyes*, Dr. Robert Keck, who has been characterized as an "evolutionary theologian," describes a developmental and interdependent process existing between animal and plant life that is comparable to our planet and universe. Using a cultural context, he pictures these processes as having three distinct Epochs. At the first evolutionary stage, Epoch I, when the human journey was still in its infancy and early childhood, he posits that there was an affinity with the mother earth. This period was characterized by cooperation rather than competition, an ecological relationship with nature rather than an exploitative one. In this period of development, the unconscious was more dominant than conscious processes. He describes it as a peaceful time where people chose living sites for beauty, as well as the accessibility of good water and soil, rather than for their inaccessibility and fortress value. He reports that during the early childhood of the race there was a notable absence of imagery idealizing war, violence or "noble warriors." Cooperation was the major modem of life. (19)

Keck suggests that during the early adolescence period, Epoch II, there has been a distinct and significant shift from the feminine to the masculine. It is a time when women lost their status as equals. It is the time where men have attempted to assert their power and virility. This period is characterized by competitiveness. Cultural authority also has shifted from the church to science. In terms of national strategies, it has been important to be the first to put "a man on the moon." During this period, astonishing advancements have been made in so many dimensions of technology, especially advances on the communication highway. Getting ahead at any cost has reflected the mentality of this era, even if getting ahead meant abandoning friends, family, and loyalties to the community. It has been a period where ethics gave way to expediency and morality gave way to what "turned you on."

When one is living in the midst of such a period, and embraces emotional and spiritual adolescence, it is difficult to get a more complete picture of what might be and to move on to the next maturational level. Many adolescent pranks, even innocent ones, can reflect a maturational lag. A story may reflect this point.

Eugene:

The rules of the fundamentalist Bible College I attended in the mid to late 40s actually characterized Catholic and other conservative church-related schools during that period. While this school was co-educational, the rules about social interaction between the sexes were very strict and rigid. Classes and chapel services were not segregated, although men and women sat in different sections. Virtually everything else was segregated, including the study hours in the library. No dates or even casual extended conversations between the sexes were permitted.

One year a 'bold' experiment was launched. Both sexes were allowed in the library at the same time between the hours of 7 and 9 p.m. The campus regulation required all students to be either in the library or in their rooms, maintaining total silence during this two-hour period.

One particular evening, I had chosen to be in my room. Being rather bored with studying, I left my room thirty minutes before the enforced study period was over. Contrary to the regulations, I wandered down the hallway of the library. Another friend, a military veteran and considerably older than I, was looking over the bulletin board in the same hallway. An impulse, typical of adolescents who were consciously or unconsciously rebelling against structure, suddenly possessed me. I pierced the silence with a loud yell, then proceeded down the hallway and pulled a fire alarm bell (which only hooked for this building) before disappearing into the night.

My friend, who had no warning of my impulsive behavior, went into a nearby-darkened classroom and hid behind the door. When caught there, he was obviously at a loss to explain his presence in the classroom since the hour had not yet arrived when he would have been free to be in the hallway. He refused to tell who had activated the alarm bell.

Meanwhile I slipped back into my room by climbing the fire escape, and appeared innocent when the Dean of Students appeared. At that developmental stage of my adolescence, confession and repentance of this behavior was not relevant. I had beat the system and felt smug.

Other examples could be cited that represent a maturational lag. To blow smoke in a person's face who is attempting to change his/her smoking behavior, or to encourage persons who are either addicted or becoming addicted, to drink or use drugs can only be described as immature behavior that is typical of adolescents who are trying to find their way.

It Doesn't Help to Hide!

Sometimes the blocks to normal development and maturation occur as a result of attempts to deal with the emptiness of our lives by what the counterculture of the 60s referred to as "turning off and tuning out."

Eugene:

A woman in her late middle years had lost her husband in death approximately a year before she was referred to me. She had just learned that her twenty-nine-year-old son had a rather aggressive form of cancer.

Her physician was concerned about the way that she seemed to be using denial inappropriately as a defense mechanism.

In asking her to contact me, he noted that I sometimes used hypnosis as a way of removing emotional blocks.

When she came to her first appointment, the first words out of her mouth were that she was a Jehovah Witness and had been taught that hypnosis was evil. She asked that I promise that I would not attempt to hypnotize her. I attempted to assure her that hypnosis was only a tool used in specific situations and then only by mutual agreement. My words, however, did not convince her. Every few minutes she sought reassurance that I was not hypnotizing her. But no amount of assurance seemed to quell her apprehension.

As her physician had suggested, there was little emotional tone in her voice. Early in our contact I attempted to elicit some moment in her life that had been filled with joy. I asked her if she could remember her wedding and the people who attended. She reported that in her mind's eye she could clearly see this event which had occurred nearly thirty-five years earlier. I asked her to remember the excitement and joy that she had felt on this occasion. She noted that she could remember the event but didn't recall any particular sense of excitement or joy.

I wondered if her long marriage had been filled with conflict and if her lack of expression could be related to a high level of ambivalence about her marriage. I then asked her to remember the birth of her son, which she clearly did. I followed by asking her to recall the sense of excitement and joy she had experienced when she first held her infant son in her arms. Again she stated that she remembered that event but didn't recall any feeling of excitement and joy.

In response I said, 'My dear lady, you have been worried about me putting you in a trance in spite of my repeated assurance that I would not do that without your permission. The truth of the matter is that you have been in a trance for thirty-five years. My job is to bring you out of that trance.'

The process of grace had been powerfully blocked in her life, with the result that she had not been able to experience the miracles that occurred all around her.

Alan Jones, the Dean of San Francisco's Grace Cathedral, comments in his book, *Passion for the Journey*, that all too many go through their days without real passion. He adds that the core passion is that we have been loved by God in an astonishing way. The baggage we are invited to jettison in the act of repentance has to do with those things which keep us from experiencing life passionately. Jones states that "repentance isn't a matter of beating our breasts and saying that deep down we're rotten. Repentance is hoping for nothing less than the truth. If we don't, we lose touch with our deepest selves, with each other and with God. Repentance—hoping for and trusting in nothing less than the truth—also means paying attention to our passion for connection. Our passion for connection is a passion for heaven. The lure of disconnection is the lure of hell."(20)

Who's on Top of the Heap?

In his book, *The Strong and the Weak*, Dr. Paul Tournier suggests that the person who plays strong or dominant roles needs others who play more needy roles. Conversely, those who play the weak role clearly feel a need for those who appear to be strong. This kind of complementary relationship is often present in marriage relationships, work places, and academic worlds as well as a host of other settings where symbiotic relationships are encouraged. When such relationships are encouraged one can be sure that the processes of grace, including repentance, will be blocked. In such relationships it is easy for one participant to feel superior to the other, and the second to consider herself/himself as the victim of the other. (21)

Carroll and Eugene:

Two young men had developed a close personal friendship. Both were talented and highly respected in the community. They had been influential and significant in each other's lives and shared a number of common interests, both in their work and social contacts. In addition, both had had a powerful emotional and spiritual experience at a weekend retreat.

One clearly played the stronger role while the other played a more passive role. From an observer's viewpoint they seemed to be inseparable. While they appeared to be supportive of each other in times of crises, one seemed to be in crisis more often.

Nevertheless, their friendship seemed as if it could survive any storm and, in fact, it lasted for a considerable length of time. Then one day their relationship ruptured in a rather dramatic way. Each felt betrayed by the other. Each saw himself as the victim and viewed the other as the victimizer, perpetuating the chasm that now divided them.

While each, in his own way, has tried to 'write the other off,' it is apparent that they are as bonded by their separation as they ever were in their togetherness. To this day, the gulf between them continues to deepen and widen. Even though years have passed since the rupture in their relationship, each appears to believe the power to bring about healing is invested in the other person. Each remains a trigger point of distress for the other.

What causes such blocks to wholeness as those manifested in this story? (+++) Can grace, inter-dependence and love exist if the basis of the relationship is dependency, or a distorted need to be needed? How does one grow to accept the strengths and the differences in another and to accept, without judgment, the other's need to be as s/he is at that moment? (+++) And from such a sense of mutual acceptance, how does one invite out that part of one's self waiting to be born? (+++)

In some respects the story of the two young men represents a microcosm for the tensions that exist between nationalities in Bosnia, Iraq, and many other parts of the world. In Bosnia and Iraq, for example, people who lived as neighbors for generations and even inter-married, now find a gulf, seemingly insurmountable, separating neighbor from neighbor, family member from family member. Where will the cycle of separation stop?

Reflections

Why do we hang on to jobs that bring us limited peace, joy and inner satisfaction? (+++) Why do we sustain marriages or other relationships that no longer feed us? (+++) What are we afraid of losing if we invite ourselves to change? (+++) Why do we put up with experiences with limited potential rather than seek those which are more potent? (+++)

Taking the Plunge!

It is a risky thing to repent, parallel in some way to a Lenten Journey that may resemble all the trauma that leads to a crucifixion. It may also, however, lead to a resurrection. Not to take the journey is to allow barriers to forgiveness to become more formidable, one's despair to deepen, and a sense of separation to hold even greater sway in the inner parts of the human spirit.

As stated earlier, repentance is often viewed as a "turning away" from a non-productive or negative behavior. We believe it to be a re-directive process, a course correction to attain one's goals and objectives. Using the language of Psychosynthess, this willing comes as a result of the "I" or Center carefully considering all options and the consequences, and then, intentionally choosing to go in a new, more self-fulfilling direction. It becomes a pro-active response. It may mean letting go of some responses we previously nurtured and moving to acquire new and untried responses. It may also mean using established behaviors in new and fresh ways.

Carroll:

As I have indicated earlier in this writing, I began my teaching at age twelve when the teacher of my one-room school in rural Ohio realized that I knew more about music than she. She invited me to become the school's music teacher. During my high school years, I was taken out my classes to teach music when either or the two regular music teachers were absent. Teaching music has been my lifelong mission.

For many years I worked daily in a supervisory capacity with teachers and students to effect music learning. When that position was eliminated, I was assigned as a principal of a school. I believe I was effective in this new role. I did find, however that much of my energy was spent on things that I did not find fulfilling. The abilities I had carefully nurtured through the years were not being used. I was doing things that others could do as well or better than I. Realizing the gifts that I had and wanted to give were still needed, I decided to take early retirement and devote my energies to sharing my gifts though writing or other means. It was a time of willing, of letting go of some of the activities that filled my time in order to make important adjustments or corrections in my life course. As the last days of my principalship drew near, I responded to a call to assist in developing an opera education program in which learners were to create and produce their own operas as a means to understanding and appreciating opera. Little did I know that the process which evolved not only supported opera but became the most integrative approach to learning that I had ever experienced.

Since 1983, I have worked with teachers and students to create and produce almost two thousand 'operatic' works in which the students write the script or libretto, compose the music, do their own auditions and casting, design their sets and costumes, perform their works and finally, often viewing the video recordings, write a review. By choosing to do things that nurtured me, I found a whole new direction for my life. The 'letting go' process (repentance) had occurred.

The Next Step

According to Keck's analysis in Sacred Eyes, referred to earlier, moving on to the next maturational level (Epoch III) is important if internal growth is to continue. He believes that we stand on the verge of moving to a time where there will be a radical shift in our awareness as a human species. The shift, he believes, will be from competition to cooperation. He speaks of the adolescence of our existence, Epoch II, not as a failure or human fault but, rather, as a symptom of a developmental stage. He adds that, in geology a "fault" is a fracture in the earth's surface and an earthquake is a violent dislocation that takes place along these faults. He adds that our developing ego created fault-lines all across the landscapes of human experience—separating heaven from earth, divine from human, matter from spirit, good from evil, humans from the rest of nature, one group of humans from other groups, and, in the individual, the separation of body, mind and spirit.

The emerging Epoch III, Keck suggests, is characterized by a synergy that does not ignore differences but sees them as part of the larger hologram; "everything participates in one grand, magnificent, mysterious, magnanimous whole." In the holistic view of the universe, everything is interrelated. In this transitional time, in this movement from reductionism to holism, we can only begin to imagine how thoroughly our inner lives are manifested in our physical and circumstantial 'fate.' While he hypothesizes that propensity toward growth is universal, persons as well as institutions can play an immensely important role in facilitating the maturational process.

A Time for Reflection and Action

Reflect on a time when you felt blocked from fully experiencing a relationship or from participation in an event. (+++). Remember and re-experience the feeling or impressions you had at the time. Note any fears you held. (+++). Were you aware of your contributions to the blocks? (+++) Think through that experience again. How you might have approached it differently? How you might have owned all the feelings. (+++) Put your ownership of those feelings and fears into words. (+++)

Chapter 5
FORGIVENESS

What's So Amazing About Forgiveness?

"Forgive them, Father, for they know not what they do."
Luke 23:34

Between the desert floor
And mountain peak
Where juniper and spiny leaf
Do intermingle,
I stopped to study
The endless variety
Of growth that clings
The rocky slope.

At first I could only see
Their pointedness
And vanity,
The way they imposed on space
As if to wrestle for their place.

But then I took a closer look
And in each saw

Beauty and uniqueness,
How they stood together
That each might flourish.

Would that humans
In all their endless variety
While struggling on their rocky slope
Learn the lesson of cactus and pine,
Accept the uniqueness of each one's gift
See the beauty deep within,
And stand together
To experience the divine.
[Carroll Rinehart]

ONE OF THE MOST POWERFUL dramas of forgiveness that captured international attention for days occurred in an Amish Community near Lancaster, Pennsylvania in October of 2006. A milkman, apparently obsessed with an experience that had occurred several decades earlier, took his revenge on a hapless group of elementary age children who were attending a rural Amish school.

After dropping off his own children at their school, he then left a cell phone message to his wife stating that he was on a mission and would not be returning home. He did the unthinkable. He entered the school and dismissed the boys and began to tie up girls. The frightened teenage schoolteacher panicked and ran for help. This action apparently disrupted his plans to molest the girls. However before any interventions could occur, he began to kill these young female students.

One of the students pleaded with the demented milkman to kill her but save her fellow classmates. However, before the carnage was over, a half dozen or more students had been killed. The gunman then turned the weapons on himself.

What happened next was unforgettable. This tight knit community, including the families whose daughters had been so cruelly murdered, quickly forgave. Their Amish Bishop explained that their theology required them to forgive. They took literally the petition in the Lord's prayer "to forgive us as we forgive." The world gasped in awe as they witnessed their forgiving behavior.

Not only did they forgive the person who committed this senseless murder, but they reached out to his widow and her children. They attended the funeral of this deeply disturbed man. They generously donated funds that would support his children. This group went the total distance in living out their faith.

Philip Yancey, in his book, *What's So Amazing About Grace?* (referred to earlier), quotes a passage from Laurens van der Post's book, *The Prisoner and the Bomb*, in which that author recalls his experiences in a Japanese prison camp in Java. Here are his words: "The only hope for the future lay in an all-embracing attitude of forgiveness of the peoples who had been our enemies. Forgiveness, my prison experience had taught me, was not merely religious sentimentality; it was as fundamental a law of the human spirit as the law of gravity. If one broke the law of gravity one broke one's neck: if one broke the law of forgiveness one inflicted a mortal wound one one's spirit and became once again a member of the chain-gang of mere cause and effect from which life has laboured so long and painfully to escape."(23)

Two paragraphs earlier, Yancey quotes Martin Luther King, Jr.: "Forgiveness is not just an occasional act; it is a permanent attitude." Yancey then adds this line: "What greater gift could Christians give to the world than the forming of a culture that upholds grace and forgiveness?"

At times we have hurtful, unsatisfying experiences. We tell ourselves that we won't allow such experiences to happen again. We hang on to the memories of the hurts. We will not let go. In consequence our actions become unfulfilling. Avoidance, revenge and other negative behaviors follow. We have negated the opportunity to become more whole.

Carroll:

I had completed the writing and the production of my first adult chancel opera—the Christmas story told from the viewpoint of the innkeeper of Bethlehem and his wife. Following the last performance of the 1992 season, a minister friend said, 'Now, can you have another opera ready for Easter?' 'Yes,' I replied, 'but it will be Easter, 1994.'

So I began my search for what I considered important to say about the crucifixion and resurrection of Jesus. Many days passed with no sense of direction for the work. However, I often pictured a gathering of the people on Golgotha and heard Jesus' words from the cross ringing in my ears, 'Forgive them, Father.'

It was during a motor trip to Phoenix from my home in Tucson that I suddenly began to think about Jesus' mother, Mary. I wondered how she must have felt coming from the crucifixion. Suddenly the words and the music filled my mind.

A mother cannot shield her child from pain.
Would that I could, if once again
There were a place to be,
Filled with grace for thee,
But alas, the time has passed
And you are gone from me.
A mother can but share her love each hour,
Within that call we share the power,
It is a gift from on high
That heals each rift forever nigh,
But alas, the time has passed
And you are gone from me.
There you hang upon the cross
A crown of thorns upon your brow
Your hands, your feet, your side drips blood.
What will happen? What will happen to us now?
There you hang upon the cross,
There you hang for all to see,
Your body, lifeless, limp, all spent,
What will happen? What will happen to me?
A mother cannot shield her child from pain.
Would that I could if once again
There were a place to be

Filled with grace for thee
But alas, the time has passed
And you are gone from me.

The central idea for the work was set. The first part addressed how various people came from the crucifixion, and how they responded to the crisis. Peter had to deal with his guilt as did the other disciples who went into hiding. A maid of no social standing encounters Peter in hiding and scornfully asks: 'Were you there when they crucified my Jesus?

Were you there when they nailed him to that tree?'
Peter replies,
'Jesus? Don't think I know him.
Don't think I know him at all.
Never met Him, as I recall.
May have seen him once or twice before
As He talked with the crowds but nothing more.
Sorry I cannot help you.'

When the woman leaves, Peter is confronted by the deceit in his denial. He recounts the denials then ends with these words: 'Forgive me, Rabbi, that I want to live.'

In the second part of the opera, the disciples and others come together in the upper room. Drawn by the meaning of their lives with Jesus, they confess and repent and, by coming together, seek and attain forgiveness. Peter begins:

'I just had to come back
I couldn't stay away.
Too many fond mem'ries of Him.
Why did we do it? Why did we all run?
Where are the rest of them?'

Peter found that, like all of us, he had to own what he had done and work through his problem:

'The memories of these past days are so painful.
I can't remember even where I've been.
Alone and in my hiding, trying to forget—
But it was of no use.
Wherever I would go He was there.'

While Carroll's opera recounts the events related to the crucifixion, it also reminds us that to experience wholeness we must be surrounded by grace, confess and own what is, repent and seek forgiveness. Where do we find ourselves in Peter's actions?

Getting Back On Track

Matthew Fox, who has written extensively of creativity and spirituality, gives this succinct definition of forgiveness in his book *Original Blessing*: "Forgiveness is another word for letting go. We are saved by the power to forgive ourselves, to allow ourselves to be forgiven, which matures into the power to forgive others and allow their time to be forgiven. Forgiveness is about letting go of guilt—some imagined, some real—about letting go of fear. There is no healing, no salvation, without forgiveness. And with forgiveness all things become saved and healed once again. Creation is restored."(24)

Eugene:

There's a dramatic story about a Methodist clergyman whose son was brutally murdered. Understandably he and his wife were overcome with grief and anger. When the murderer was found guilty and sentenced, the minister later stated that, at the time of sentencing, no punishment would have been too severe. In time, he began to sense some incongruence with the deep anger and resentment that he held toward the person who murdered his son and the values related to forgiveness which he professed to hold and often articulated from the pulpit. As the tension resulting from this internal contradiction began to grew, he eventually knew that he needed to take action to relieve the uneasiness that was plaguing him. He clearly was not ready, however, to forgive this person for his wretched behavior.

He came to the conclusion that he needed to come face-to-face with the murderer if he were going to find a measure of peace. Eventually a meeting was arranged at the prison. He was filled with apprehension as well as great deal of ambivalence as he made his way to this encounter.

Something unexpected happened during this meeting. He began to see this young man, not as the hardened criminal who had murdered his son, but as a person made in the image of God. At some point in the interview, he was shocked to hear his own words: 'I forgive you.' In that moment, the heavy burden of resentment lifted and he sensed an internal peace that he hadn't known in a long time. He recognized that his only real choice was to forgive. Not to forgive would have meant a slow form of death.

He and his wife, in time, petitioned the State in which they were living to pardon and release the man who had 'snuffed out' the life of their son. This young man was eventually returned to the community. But there is more to the story. They appeared together in a number of different forums to speak about the healing power of forgiveness and reconciliation. In many respects, the story parallels the story lines of the opera that Carroll describes earlier in this chapter.

What are some of the factors (subtle and otherwise) that block the process of forgiveness? Why do we so often feel dissatisfied with ourselves and out of touch with others? Obviously satisfactory responses to these questions are complex.

In his book, *Assessing Moral Development*, the Harvard psychologist Lawrence Kohlberg has provided an important conceptual basis for understanding how a person develops a moral and ethical framework to guide behavior. He speaks of different stages of moral development. In the early stages the child imitates the moral/ethical system of its parents or some significant other. This stage is highly concrete and other directed. As children grow and develop they become more process oriented and inner directed. However, this normal progression can be blocked much in the same way that physical or emotional maturation can be blocked. For example, if one's adult models respond to crisis or conflict in much the same way they did at age ten, it will seriously limit the range of more mature and functional responses to crisis that would be desirable for a child to learn. (25)

Let's consider the following: the more rigid conceptual patterns a person has developed, the less open that person will be to accepting another person as he/she is. Releasing from a transcending rigidity (resulting in enhanced levels of spiritual maturation) is needed before forgiveness can be achieved.

Eugene:

There is a story about a female missionary who was stationed in Ecuador. She came from a theological perspective that clearly divided people into the saved and lost. Consistent with this position, for twenty years she prayed daily for her lost brother. On one of these prayerful occasions, she experienced a powerful realization. Her description of what happened is deeply touching, 'As I was praying, it suddenly occurred to me to thank God for my brother just as he was.' She attributed this awakening to the guidance of the Holy Spirit who, in her view, had transcended a system of tightly bound theological thought. From Kohlberg's perspective, she passed from a low level to a higher level of ethical and moral development quickly and dramatically. She reports that soon after this change in her perspective—a change which she had not conveyed to her brother, he had a profound conversion experience.

This missionary probably did not change the essential content of her religious convictions. However, her release from the rigid ritual she had practiced for twenty years freed her to think, see, feel and act in more mature ways. Perhaps her developmental growth spurt was a kind of conversion in itself even though she had not realized her own need to be saved from rigidity. Transformations of this nature are truly graceful and lead to the process of forgiveness and healing.

Kohlberg's stages of development can be perverted to result in feelings of arrogance. If **A** assumes to have progressed to higher levels and considers **B** to be at a lower level, then it would be easy to attribute superiority on moral and ethical matters to **A**. Such an unfounded assumption undoubtedly could create a gap in communication between **A** and **B**.

Without discarding Kohlberg's instructive model, consider this alternative hypothesis. Communication gaps that result in dysfunctional ways of relating between people derive from those peoples' different life experiences and different cultural understandings of the world. How can such differences be bridged? (+++) How can forgiveness be experienced, particularly if there is no way to prove one set of conceptualizations superior to others? (+++)

Carroll:

Several years ago I was directing a church choir. Having to prepare several anthems for inclusion in the service each week was sometimes very satisfying, but at other times less desirable. One Sunday the choir was not adequately prepared to sing the announced anthem. Too much time had been spent on preparing a major work to be performed two weeks later. The choir valiantly struggled through the anthem, but, as director, I felt unfulfilled by the experience.

My internal 'critical judge' berated me and laid the total blame for the sub-standard performance at my feet. I was hurting, but functional, as I went off to a small committee meeting following the church services. When I arrived at the meeting room, I was confronted directly by a young man from the University who eagerly pointed out my failings related to the anthem. Imagine how that reinforced my 'critical judge.'

As this was occurring, we were joined by two pastors who, sensing my discomfort, jumped to my defense, reminding me of the inordinate number of times I had been very successful, that my 'batting average' was extremely high. Now that was 'music' to the ear of my 'creative' sub-personality. However, an inner argument ensued that, within three hours, totally immobilized me, making it impossible for me to provide services at an afternoon function.

A short role-playing session in which my warring sub-personalities talked to each other and gathered perspective brought me back to a functioning base rather quickly. The questions that lingered for me were about my need to strive for perfection, to be the perfect '10,' and my willingness to assign undue authority and power to others to judge me and what I do. I also noted my ability to simply accept the experience as a part of the flow of life—a flow in which the spirit does not solely reside in rhythmic perfection.

Reflections

Identify a time in your life when you were able to release from a non-productive pattern of thinking or being. (+++) As you reflect on it now, what were the crucial elements of change? (+++)

We're all in the same boat

The world population is in a struggle between the role and relationship of the "haves" and the "have-nots." Struggles exist between the opposing views of liberals and conservatives, Middle Eastern Arabs and Jews, Irish Catholics and Protestants; conflicts, also, regarding our military role in Iraq and Afghanistan and between the "right to life" and the "right to choice" positions of people the world-over.

Other examples of similar struggles from everyday life can readily surface particularly in those areas that are 'hot buttons' for individuals. For example, when someone aggressively asks "Have you been born again?" it is easy for the listener to become defensive, especially if the question connotes that the questioner feels she or he has fully 'arrived.'

Openness is a crucial element in the process of forgiveness. With the "Have you been born again?" question, it is important that defensiveness give way to authentic dialogue between the principals. It is not a win/lose situation, not a matter for one person to overpower the other. When an encounter is viewed as one more battle to win or one more trophy to capture, the process of forgiveness is thwarted. Such encounters become even more complicated when those involved have a history of unresolved conflicts.

A common response to the question, "Have you been born again?" leads to verbal abuse and disdain for the questioner. An alternative response such as: "I can understand that being born again has a very special meaning to you, but I see this dynamic in a much broader perspective." While this response seems smoother, it also blocks authentic dialogue. As innocent and empathetic as a declaration like this may seem, it presumes that the speaker's understanding has much greater depth and substance than the questioner, whose truth is narrow, shallow, unsophisticated and easy to 'write off.' In effect, the person who appears to have taken the high road has responded in kind to the person posing the "born again" question, albeit in a smoother and perhaps less offensive way.

If forgiveness is to occur, one must be willing to enter into significant dialogue, sometimes at great risk. Such risk involves accepting the radical imperative of Jesus' dictum, "Judge not, that ye be not judged, for judgment is mine saith the Lord."

Barriers to Forgiveness

There are a number of barriers that prevent forgiveness from occurring. More often than not, the person with whom we experience barriers is not that overbearing individual whom we barely know. It is more often a person who touches our lives in many ways.

Eugene:

I tend to see things from a sweeping philosophical and global perspective that looks past many of the smaller details. Conversely, my wife tends to be more concrete and is aware of those details I barely notice. I confess that I often experience irritation when she wants to deal with these details while I impatiently want to go on to larger things. While these larger things seem clear enough to me, she feels confused because many of the details important to her have not been attended to. When I judge concrete things to be too mundane to deal with, she often feels unheard and de-valued. The differences in our individual roles, perceptions and priorities make it difficult to move toward forgiveness and healing when these attitudes get activated between us.

Stumbling Over More Blocks

There seem to be at least three major stumbling blocks to the process of forgiveness. First, there are problems in communication which often reflect differences in the levels of communication and variations in language usage. For example, one person, in the process of communicating, may be operating at a very concrete level while the other person is functioning at a metaphoric or abstract level. The result is that they are likely to miss each other.

A second block to forgiveness is often a lack of congruity between the forgiveness one experiences from oneself and that which one may receive from another. One may be forgiven by someone else but be unable to forgive oneself or vice versa. Forgiveness leading to reconciliation is not an option; it is the key to wholeness and sustained growth.

A third block to forgiveness occurs when we fail to internalize the values we confess. It is difficult to see gray if one polarizes and sees only black and white.

Reflections

Remember a time in your life when you experienced some small hurt or embarrassment that went unresolved. And, as you held on to the experience, it seemed to fester and grow. (+++) You may have even forgotten what it was all about. The longer it remained unresolved, the more difficult it was to own. With this awareness, you may want to make the change that you need now. You can ask for forgiveness of the other person, if that is your need, or you can seek forgiveness within yourself. (+++)

It is easy to think of evil as dark sinister forces 'out there,' but it is much more difficult to see similar sinister forces within ourselves. For example, violence in our society is a concern that needs to be addressed. However, to authentically explore violence from this perspective, it will be necessary to start by examining the propensity for violence within ourselves. We may abhor shoplifting yet copy, without guilt, materials created and owned by others. The following experience illustrates the limiting perspective of a 'black and white' orientation.

Eugene:

I'm not sure why I was so timid and shy during the early decades of my life. All my siblings seemed to have escaped such a behavioral limitation. In my view, my father, who carried his own maturational burdens, tried to compensate for his lack of self esteem by developing a strongly authoritarian way of being. As a growing child, I did not dare to challenge him in any way. The result was that I became overly compliant to him and to authority figures of any kind.

From a pacifistic background, it is somewhat surprising that I was to be first in my family, although not the last, to voluntarily enter military service. Even though I became a part of an elite airborne division and fully participated in the vigorous training necessary for this assignment, I remained essentially a pacifist in my heart.

While stationed in Europe, I was assigned to an infantry division that spent a great deal of time on military maneuvers. I volunteered for more than my share of field duty. Beyond wanting to conscientiously serve my unit as its chaplain, my need to please governed a lot of my actions. At the same time, I was very uneasy around military authority figures. As a result, I tended to avoid the headquarters offices. My two chaplain colleagues, on the other hand, spent a great deal of time competing for the commander's attention and, thus, were frequent visitors to headquarters.

I reasoned that as the junior chaplain in rank I would do my best *to be visible among the troops and attempt to build a rapport with them. On one occasion, with little training or preparation, I agreed to go on a twenty-five mile overnight forced march with one of our companies The colonel, who commanded our unit, heard of my participation in this event. Later, to my utter surprise, I found myself in the role of the favorite chaplain, even though I was junior in rank and not Roman Catholic.*

Shortly after, the officers of the entire unit had a major festive event at the Officers' Club. The uniform was dress blues and attendance was required. In those days, 'hard drinking' was in. As a 'tee-totaler,' I quickly lost the ability to have rational conversation with my fellow officers who were rapidly moving toward inebriation.

The colonel, who had been a wrestler at West Point, was a big man with a large capacity for alcohol. He spotted me and engaged me in friendly conversation—his speech slurred. While I certainly valued his approval, I was also very frightened of him. Dozens of officers would have loved the attention he gave me that night. However, I didn't realize until much later, when my fears had abated, how lonely he was. Because of my panic, I hadn't been able to be present to him. I hadn't realized that the fear I had of my father had transferred to this moment. I had missed an opportunity for healing with the colonel and, vicariously, with my father.

Forgiveness has no limits

National periodicals and local news media increasingly focus on the dramatics and the need for forgiveness. It seems to reflect the need for forgiveness in order to achieve more wholeness. It has been an important element of the national men's organization, the "Promise Keepers."

Eugene:

I had just completed a sermon on the topic of forgiveness. One of the points I had emphasized was the importance of forgiving oneself. After the sermon one of the parishioners asked whether Susan Smith, the South Carolina mother who had strapped her two young sons into their car seats and, then, allowed the car to roll off the dock into the lake, should forgive herself.

After a brief lapse of a few seconds, I responded 'Absolutely! That's what the Gospel is about!' What was the cause of my delayed response? Was I concerned about upsetting the parishioner? Was I simply running the question through my internal computer? Or did I have a flicker of doubt about whether there are limits on grace?

Getting it together

For many people, a lack of integration between forgiving oneself, and accepting forgiveness offered by someone else, is a major block to achieving wholeness.

Our own internal judges, who constantly critique us and require us to meet rigorous standards and quality levels, can often be harsher on us than others from whom we seek forgiveness. Meeting one's own expectations can be very demanding. When our expectations are not met, we are likely to experience pain, guilt, embarrassment or some other form of personal discomfort.

The critical judge's seeming indictment "There you did it again! You dummy! What will people think?" only make matters worse. The pain derived from being criticized registers internally and takes massive doses of support to overcome and resolve. One can consciously and intellectually contend that all is well, but one's internal state can be quite different. The internal judge may well be saying "You really have to be on guard to make sure that this doesn't happen again. You can't stand that kind of pain and embarrassment!" While the internal judge may have good intentions, it is important to move beyond the defensive position to a centered, holistic position in order to experience forgiveness.

The world is populated with groups who are sure they have discovered the whole truth. Critics are made of such "knowers!" Even so, it is also important to remember that no two persons attending the same theater event or concert, or the same church service, come away having seen and/or heard the same things. Our perceptions, colored by previous experiences, modify and distort reality, limiting our ability to definitely "know" what is presented. When attending a large banquet, our prior experiences with food will shape our appreciations for the foods set before us. Knowledge of health practices and the impact of certain "unhealthy" foods upon our bodies can also shape our appreciations of a feast.

Carroll:

I am a Type 2 diabetic. Food in our family was a part of all family celebrations. The women of the family were wonderful cooks. The food products from our family farm were highly caloric and plentiful. Working on the farm burned calories efficiently. Except for a few members of the family, all handled the abundance reasonably well.

Once removed from the farm, my appetite for plenteous, rich food continued. Hard, physical work was no longer my pattern, and abundance turned into weight beyond desirable norms for me.

In my seventy-first year I was diagnosed as a diabetic. I was to greatly reduce the consumption of fats and sugars. The amount of my food intake changed little. When going out to dinner I would generously partake of the breads brought to the table, then ask for more. My medications were doubled and taken to maximum dosages.

My diabetic problem remained. Then the doctor said, 'You have a choice. Either get your weight down and your sugar under control or we begin insulin injections.' These options provided me with an easy choice. I began to eat to live, reduced my weight twenty-five pounds in three months, and reduced the required medication by one-half. I realized I had begun to alter a life-long pattern of eating without reducing my enjoyment of food.

When I was an undergraduate in college, I attended a relatively small but excellent school whose roots were grounded in a conservative religious tradition. Dancing was 'evil' as perceived by the church and was forbidden on campus. Nothing was said, however, if one went to a bar and danced or attended dances off campus.

The school, through its music department, stressed rhythmic responses to music, the release of energy through music, and one's ability to respond to the musical rhythmic elements. Students seeking natural social relationships and pleasurable activities were placed in a conflict between the inconsistent values of the college and their inner selves.

As we have said earlier, each of us possesses a variety of sub-personalities. These learned or acquired patterns of behavior, initially there for good purpose, do at times fail to serve the greater well-being.

Meet More Internal Family Members

From a Psychosynthesis frame of reference, many of us have a personal historian. This sub-personality keeps a running record of our hurts and celebrations. It keeps reminding us that given certain conditions we can expect to be hurt again. Celebrations remind us of the conditions under which we have experienced pleasure in the past—a filter that the historian can use in the future to create the proper set and setting for additional celebrations. The problem is that the historian may subvert the intent of the individual and begin to avoid situations in which the person can move toward a greater sense of wholeness.

Carroll:

As a child of six, long before I knew much about sex, I had a negative sexual experience with older boys. The result was that I was laughed at and made to feel inadequate. Shortly after when visiting neighbors, their little girl who was my age, dropped her panties and said, 'I'll show you mine if you show me yours!'

I panicked. Our playtime ended. But for many years memories of that experience haunted me. And even when intellectually I was aware of my own sexual adequacy, I still had to work through the emotional part of the memory. My personal historian was difficult to fully re-program, and update.

Many of us have an accuser sub-personality, an attacker of others. Accusers are very prone to want to shift responsibility away from themselves to avoid dealing with real issues. From a lay person's point of view, the current finger-pointing by both political parties on the issue of campaign contributions seems to be a blatant example of trying to "make political hay" rather than attempting creatively to find a solution to campaign financing. It is interesting to note that those who most loudly accuse their opponents are not willing to take the risk to modify the system. Apparently, accusers are not willing, themselves, to change a system from which they glean benefits.

From a Psychosynthesis perspective, such behavior comes from a self serving sub-personality and not from the integrative Center.

All the sub-personalities outlined above share a common thread—avoidance! It is easy to walk away from something and not have to deal with it. However, there is a price to pay for avoidance. Problems are not resolved simply by walking away.

Carroll:

Several years ago, while employed in the Tucson Unified School District, I was teaching music through the medium of television. It was in the early days of instructional television and, due to strict budget restraints, there was never time for adequate planning or rehearsal. Often the teaching was done without rehearsal. On one such day things had not gone well. I came away from the studio with a strong sense of failure. I berated myself for having allowed such things to happen, although in reflecting back upon the day I could not remember any details of what went wrong! Wearily I headed back toward my office.

On my way, I decided to take refuge in the cafeteria to have a cup of coffee to soothe my negative emotions. Seated in the cafeteria were several of my peers from other curriculum areas. One had seen the telecast and sarcastically greeted me with, 'Had a rough day, huh?' Other things were said in a critical manner. My already wounded self only cut more deeply into my consciousness. Holding onto my hurts, I retreated from the cafeteria to cry silently.

I never did share that afternoon experience with my friend. I never let him know that his negative comments had added to my sense of woundedness. For many years our relationship limped along. Frequently, I simply avoided him. What could have been a very rich relationship for us never really developed. During those years I expect he must have wondered what had happened to cause the distance in our relationship.

Contrast that with another experience in the same school district. The setting was an administrative meeting in which the Associate Superintendent was present. I was with my peers and the people to whom I reported. Although I don't recall the specific comments that were made, I do remember that at one point the Associate Superintendent, with whom I had a very friendly relationship, directed a comment to me. He had intended it to be funny and spontaneous. To me, however, it was received as a 'put-down' which hurt. For a few seconds the people around the table fell silent. An awkwardness prevailed. Then I said 'Wow, that hurt. I don't know what to do with it!' My friend immediately responded, 'I intended it to be funny. When I started to speak I knew it wasn't what I had intended to say, but I couldn't seem to get it stopped! I'm sorry!' There was an immediate relaxation around the table. My friend and I looked at each other, smiled in acceptance, and the work continued. Everyone felt okay about how we had resolved the miscommunication that had occurred between us.

What is the difference between the two stories? In the first, I had failed to acknowledge my hurt and to confess. Because I avoided the confession, the action of repentance could not occur. My historian had taken over, thinking it was being helpful. By avoiding the problem, it had negated the possibility for forgiveness and wholeness to evolve.

In the second story, my immediate confession and the implied need for repentance made forgiveness a most natural outcome. By owning my feelings, acknowledging what was true for me at that moment, I provided the opportunity to heal the moment and move on.

When grace or unconditional acceptance is present, confession is more readily achieved. Trust can be more fully present. When we own the condition, we set the stage to let go and move to repentance. Without willing or wanting to change, there is little need for forgiveness.

Time for Reflection

Remember a time when you felt unforgiven by someone or when you could not forgive yourself for some word or action. (+++) How did you experience the lack of forgiveness? (+++) What was happening in your body? (+++) What level of energy did you feel? (+++). How did you relate to others socially? (+++) Was your ability to get things done compromised? If so, how? (+++) What was the basis of the problem? (+++) Did you own your feelings?

(+++) Did you share them? How? With whom? (+++) Did you make any decisions to let them go? (+++) Did you eventually do it? What did you feel after sharing? (+++)

Now think of a time when you experienced feeling hurt and were able to own your hurt to others (confession), then let it go (repentance). (+++) How did you experience forgiveness, from others or yourself? How was it reflected in the responses of your body? (+++) How was it reflected in your ability to relate to others? (+++) How was it reflected in your sense of energy and inspiritedness in your life? (+++)

When you experience negative energies, write about what you are thinking, feeling, doing—what is transpiring around you. Consider whether there is a state of grace (unconditional acceptance) in your relationships; consider your ability to own or confess your state of being; think about your desire to take appropriate action to resolve it, and note whether, within yourself, you have a willingness to forgive yourself and others as needed. (+++)

Chapter 6
RECONCILIATION

Hallelujah, It's All Changed!

I held your hand
And felt the history of man.
Within that grasp
We linked
All history
to
Eternity
[Carroll Rinehart]

SOME MOMENTS ARE SO DRAMATIC, so graceful, so healing that they continue to be compelling long after the powerful moment has passed. One such moment occurred just hours before a friend, Jenny's, granddaughter was to be married.

Eugene:

When the granddaughter was barely a toddler, her mother had abandoned her father, taking their only child with her, and disappeared from sight. Years passed before she, the daughter, was to have contact with her father and grandmother. After this reunion she continued to have contact with her divorced parents, although the parents had not seen each other for nearly twenty years.

The rage the father experienced due to the 'abduction' of his daughter by her mother had subsided with the passing years. After re-establishing contact with his daughter he felt considerable resolution. However, he continued to harbor a great deal of resentment toward his ex-spouse.

A moment of drama and grace came when the mother, now living in a Southern state, arrived at the home of her ex-husband's aunt in the city where the daughter's marriage was to take place. She came alone knowing that her ex-husband, also from a distant city, was waiting for her with their daughter, the perspective groom, his mother and other members of his extended family. The ex-wife obviously wondered how she would be received. Her anxiety must have been 'sky high.'

I was with the family as they waited in the livng room for the bride's mother to arrive. We heard the sound of a taxi arriving in the street, followed by the closing of a car door. We could hear her footsteps coming up the walkway, up the wooden steps and then across the front porch to the front door.

All of us virtually frozen. It seemed as if our breathing had stopped. I know I was scarcely breathing. The seconds before the doorbell rang seemed forever. The heartbeat of the bride's mother must have been racing and her body trembling.

After the ring of the doorbell, there was a long hesitation. No one moved. Then the ex-husband finally went to answer the door. The couple looked into each other's eyes for the first time in twenty years. There was an agonizing moment when neither spoke. He then opened his arms and they embraced. There wasn't a dry eye in the room. Two decades of hurt, pain and anger melted away in a single moment. Healing of a profound nature took place within that simple embrace.

While each former spouse had formed new families and developed separate histories, this powerful moment of grace transcended their broken relationship. In that moment of reconciliation, they were able to bless the marriage of their daughter.

What Changed?

We have reflected on the conditions necessary for confession, repentance, forgiveness and reconciliation to occur. We have concluded that a sense of presence, an individual's commitment to be here-and-now in the moment, is a key element for a graceful moment to occur. In the drama just described, it is doubtful that the healing would have occurred if this estranged couple had not taken the risk to forgo their histories with each other to take full advantage of their immediate experience of reunion.

In the story above, one component of this presence undoubtedly had something to do with the common bond that each parent had with their daughter. Yet that bond, in and of itself, had not been enough to override the estrangement they had maintained for two decades. Something more had to occur to facilitate a deeper level of recognition of the power of their continuing bonds with each other. Certainly the importance of rituals and time honored ceremonies cannot be over-estimated in the raising of awareness. As powerful as ceremonies can be in providing a context for creating a new level of consciousness, these events alone are often not enough to provide a context for the graceful moment to occur. Examples abound where families, who could have been gracefully blessed by special sensitive moments, have only deepened the emotional and spiritual ravines which estranged them from the significant others in their lives and ultimately from themselves.

In the experience just described, both the mother and father had chosen to move on into new relationships and create more complete lives. Reflect for a moment on how the fullness of their new relationship may have contributed to their reconciliation. (+++) Would reconciliation have been possible if either or both had chosen to turn their respective hurts and experiences of separation into lifestyles of resentment and vengefulness? In what way has your own experience of holding on to hurts blocked your reconciliation or your renewal and ability to function more fully? (+++)

A Sacramental Moment

When one is open, consciously or unconsciously, to moments of grace, the results are often dramatic.

Eugene:

As a military reservist, on one occasion I was a Chaplain on duty at Tripler Hospital in Honolulu. It was my first assignment there, and I was placed 'on call' the night of the day I arrived. The hospital was being renovated and some of the passage ways were closed. For a newcomer, it was mass confusion to go from one location to another. On this particular night, there were a number of calls requesting the services of a Chaplain. One such call came at 2 a.m. from the Neo-natal Emergency room that served new-born babies and their mothers.

As soon I arrived, the young doctor on duty took me aside and informed me that it was unlikely that one of the newborns would survive and her parents wanted to have her baptized. It turned out that the mother was Korean, spoke almost no English, and likely had no Christian background. Her husband was a black soldier from a Baptist religious tradition. On the surface, it hardly seemed that a Christian infant baptism was appropriate. Yet it became a powerful moment.

The infant was lying naked on a medical table with a number of life support systems hooked up to her tiny body. My first reaction was that, with all these attachments, it was going to be difficult to find a spot on her body to place my hand after I had dipped into the baptism bowl. The mother, still very sore from a difficult delivery, had come with her husband to the nurses station where the infant was to be baptized. As I placed my hand on this fragile child, I noticed that the two doctors and two nurses were also placing their hands on the parents. The moment was electrifying. In that moment it didn't matter which faith the participants embraced. What we realized was that we were in the presence of the Giver of Life was with us in that very special, sacramental moment. We stood in the very presence of the mystery of life itself.

After the ceremony, one of the doctors stated that he wanted to examine the child once more. After a moment, he announced that the child had no chance to live. Hence, he recommended that the child be removed from the life support systems, wrapped in a blanket, and placed in her parent's arms for as long as she lived. The two doctors, two nurses and I surrounded this young couple as the baby's life slowly ebbed away, ushering this little one into the presence of God. That sacramental moment will be forever etched in my memory.

Many Bridges to Reconciliation

While one of the authors was in the Middle East on an Educational Opportunities Study Tour, a colleague shared a moving story during morning meditations. It focused on a Jewish psychiatrist by the name of Enoch and a Palestinian writer by the name of Raja. Enoch and Raja had met fortuitously at the time Prime Minister Sadat of Egypt made his historic address to the Knesett in Israel. A university had arranged for some Israeli and Palestinian professionals and students to have an interchange of responses, in a classroom, following Sadat's speech. It was hoped that these two groups of thoughtful people might bridge the vast differences in their histories, cultures and respective agendas for the future of the area.

Something powerful occurred that neither Enoch nor Raja would have anticipated. A transformational experience caught them both by surprise. They had difficulty explaining what had occurred and found themselves alone in that classroom long after everyone else had left. Even though they were deeply entrenched in their own respective histories, they were seeing each other through new eyes.

What was it that helped them see each other with new eyes? Raja's observation is perhaps a key to understanding their transformative experience. (26)

"We began as personal friends and slowly, as our trust in each other grew, we faced up to, and confronted each other with, the feelings that we each have as members of our warring peoples. This has often been difficult, but so far has only deepened our friendship. It is not only Enoch's gentleness, and far-flung imagination and knowledge, that comes out in the way he loves our land. It is also his freedom from fears that stamp both Arabs and Jews. Enoch does not expect me to forget, when we laugh and walk together, nor does he forget himself, the accumulation through the years of the wrongs that his people have done to mine no more than I expect him to forget the terrible sufferings of his people. Like many Palestinians, I used to see it as inevitable that the survivors of the Holocaust would be driven by such hate and fear that they would act ruthlessly to ensure their own preservation, regardless of who paid for it. But Enoch remembers the evil perpetrated against his people, remembers it deeply, without himself being a hate-blinded, vengeance-seeking victim of that wrong. In him I see that really honoring the memory of people who have suffered created courage and a capacity for love that cannot be equaled by someone who does not acknowledge man's capacity for evil."

This deeply spiritual shift changed their respective worldviews, and the way each thought. More importantly, it deeply impacted the way they were to live out their lives. Deep levels of trust, that neither would have thought possible, began to develop between them. They were able to see the pain that each culture had inflicted on the other. Each began to feel, at the deepest levels of awareness, the alienation the other culture had experienced. Both were in touch with their deepest longings for reconciliation. While each was undeniably rooted in his own history, each longed for something more--a profound cultural healing that would bridge deeply ingrained internalized messages of suspicion and hate that were centuries old. Raja speaks of choosing this third way as an alternative to mute submission or blind hate. He rightly observed that states of mind cannot be forced on people.

"Your mind is the one thing that you can prevent your oppressor from having the power to touch."

Jesus said basically the same thing when he instructed his followers to love their enemies. (27) Such love appears to have drawn Raja and Enoch together, despite their very different histories and cultural backgrounds. Love in action is fundamental to the process of reconciliation.

Actions Speak Louder than Words

An Anglo farm couple from Northern California lived an honorable but simple life style. Although not vocal people, they lived out their conviction that all of life is sacred. In many respects they were far ahead of their times. In the midst of the war hysteria in the United States, especially following Japan's bombing of Pearl Harbor, our national leaders were expecting our western shores to be invaded by the Japanese. The drastic action of herding people of Japanese background into what essentially were concentration camps seemed logical at the time. Seen from our contemporary vantage point, however, this was one of the most embarrassing chapters of our involvement in that war.

We now know that the overwhelming majority of these American citizens with Japanese ancestry had a strong loyalty to their adopted homeland and to the Stars and Stripes. With little or no evidence, the entire ethnic group had been branded as a national security risk, even though many Japanese-American families had come to the United States generations ago to live out their dreams and be free people.

Without notice, they had been forced to leave established businesses and homes to live in an environment where they were guarded by soldiers and were treated as prisoners of war. Elderly grandparents, along with middle-aged couples and young families and their children, were uprooted, leaving them no financial basis to maintain their places of business during the lengthy internment.

Valuable farms were confiscated by the government and sold at public auction for taxes. Many land-hungry farmers eagerly purchased these properties that rightly belonged to the interned Japanese-Americans who were victimized by a fate over which they were powerless.

The modest Anglo farm couple, alluded to above, lived out their faith in an exciting but quiet way. They went to the County court buildings and, out of their own pockets, paid the taxes on a number of Japanese-American farms to prevent them from falling into other hands. They apparently didn't publicize their actions to anyone. But when the rightful owners of these farms were released from the internment camps, and came back to find their farms intact, their gratitude to this couple who had remained inconspicuous was deep seated, intense and profound.

In the years to come, for as long as this couple lived, they were given a very special seat of honor whenever Japanese-Americans had a celebration. Weddings and other festive events gave these grateful people an opportunity to remember their Anglo friends' actions of compassion and kindness. Their acts of reconciliation were instrumental in releasing old hurts and healing old wounds.

Surprised by Joy

A friend and colleague, the Reverend Dr. David Wilkinson, tells a story that gets at the heart of the process of reconciliation. While traveling in the Middle East as a student on a limited budget, he caught a train in Cairo to go to Luxor, the "City of the Gods." He was quick to discover that there were significant price differences between the three classes of accommodations on the train and chose the cheapest, the third class. What he didn't realize, however, was that third class cars had no seats and no service of any kind. On journeys taking a number of hours, passengers were expected to bring their own food.

After boarding, he quickly noted that groups of people were sitting on the floor. As the only non-Arab in the car, he felt isolated and alone, and very frightened. Stereotypic stories he had heard about Arab thievery, and worse, rushed to his mind, filling him with apprehension and anxiety. He found a corner and huddled there by himself. Being the only non-native in this car, he obviously stood out. He noticed that he was being eyed by one of the groups sitting on the floor, which, he confesses, further terrified him until he was virtually immobilized. One of the members of the group that was watching him motioned for him to join them. David could only shake his head "no" and wonder why he had placed himself in such a precarious situation.

His refusal, however, didn't discourage this group from making further overtures toward him. They showed him a piece of bread, and continued to motion for him to join them. Thinking that he was being set up, he refused to budge. Then an older man came to him, continuing to offer him a piece of bread until David became aware that he was being invited to join the group in their meal. Somewhat cautiously, David followed the man to his group and, after a few moments of initial awkwardness, the tension began to dissolve. Even though they had no common language, David began to understand that their gestures of friendship were genuine. Soon there was laughter and sharing that simply defied the language barrier. David then realized he was celebrating the bread and the wine with them much like that shared at the Eucharist, at Holy Communion.

What's the Test?

How does one know that reconciliation has truly occurred? Obviously this question has many dimensions. Such comments as, "the grass looked greener," "the sky looked brighter" or "there was a spring in my heel" are common expressions signaling a significant experiential shift. There is also a sense in which boundaries of reality change. Dynamic changes occur almost in a kaleidoscopic way.

Eugene:

Several years ago I went through an experience called the Walk to Emmaus. This event grew out of the Roman Catholic 'Crusillo' in Spain. While it didn't require physical exercise, it did involve profound spiritual exercises. For me, it was one of those rare experiences where in the midst of what seemed to be ordinary, something of a very 'inordinate' shift occurred. I was truly caught by 'inspiriting' surprises.

I probably would not have attended this event except for the fact that two valued colleagues, both clergy who had had a long confrontational history with each other, had experienced a profound healing of their troubled relationship as a result of their mutual participation in the Emmaus event.

Because I trusted them both, valued their judgments, and had been moved by the transforming nature of their experience, I decided it would be worthwhile to invest my time and energy in this seventy-two hour event.

Some months prior to my Walk to Emmaus, there had been a great deal of tension in my marriage. While I cared for my wife, and she for me, I was no longer willing to stay in a marriage that evidenced so little energy. The issue was not determining who was at fault. From my perspective, I didn't want to contribute to a situation that I experienced as mostly lifeless. My decision to leave had come after several years of struggle.

I went to the Walk willing to look at my decision, but not really planning to change it. The decision had been too painful. It had been made in the face of my ethic which suggested that one doesn't back away from any commitment, most certainly not the commitment of marriage.

About mid-way through this seventy-two hour experience, I began to question what my friends found so powerful. I had heard a number of speeches that sounded fairly conservative if not dogmatic. Up to this point, however, nothing in the experience had led me to believe that it would be a life-altering event.

On Saturday, early in the afternoon, I was caught by total surprise. I began to experience an intensity of caring that I had only previously known on rare occasions. To say that I was overwhelmed would have been an understatement.

Among the expressions of caring, referred to by this community as 'agape' was a letter from my brother, who lived in Alabama, that caught me by surprise. He had experienced a Crusillo event some years earlier. I had no idea how he knew that I was on this retreat. I was so moved by my brother's letter, which unbeknown to me had been solicited by the leaders of the Walk to Emmaus, that I wanted to weep.

My childhood training had suggested that for a male to weep openly is feminine and shows weakness. Nevertheless, there was an enormous lump in my throat and tears in my eyes that I could barely restrain. For long moments I sat there as if in a stupor before daring to open my brother's letter, fearful that whatever residual controls I had left would evaporate.

There was also a letter from our youngest son, who later became a United Methodist minister. Like my brother's agape letter, our son's words were warm and appreciative. In that moment, I was fully in touch with the power of my human connections.

From that moment forward, I was no longer the detached observer analyzing the contents of the instructional material. I eagerly looked forward to that which would happen next.

Some hours passed and those of us who were called Pilgrims were totally surprised again by a touching candlelight service, hosted by those who had previously been on an Emmaus Walk. They abundantly showered us with their love and songs of faith as we walked down the aisles of the church sanctuary.

Later in the evening, after all of those who received us with their songs and their love mysteriously vanished, we were prepared to experience deeply moving confessional moments of healing. We were invited to 'let go' of all that blocked our sense of union with God and our union with each other. It was here that I confessed the brokenness of our marriage, to a person whom I would not have chosen as confessor, and asked for healing. Healing did, in fact, occur but not in the way which I would have anticipated. I had expected that my wife and I would choose different paths but would learn to love each other in a new way, different from continuing as husband and wife.

For weeks after this experience, I was afraid to give up the idea of separation for fear that we would simply revert to our old ways of being. If either were to revert to old behaviors, I wasn't sure that I would be able to muster the courage to again make the critical decision to separate.

My wife went through the Walk to Emmaus shortly after I did. She also had a powerful experience that was as meaningful for her as mine had been for me. One day, subsequent to our respective Walks, all of the energy I had invested in leaving my marriage simply vanished. I was no longer afraid of what might happen at some future time.

Several decades have now passed. Have I had regrets about not following through on the decision to leave? Sometimes. Have we fallen in the same old rut in our relationships? Often. Was it the right decision for me to stay? Clearly it was, although frequently communication is strained between us. Has reconciliation fully occurred? No. Was it worth it to take the risk to stay? Yes. Have there been moments when, in the midst of being stuck in old behavioral ruts, I have questioned the wisdom of reconsidering my decision to leave? Yes. While my wife may frame her questions about our relationship somewhat differently, her questions are certainly as legitimate as any that I might raise.

Using the sub-personality framework, one might ask which sub-personality prevented the initial reconciliation from maturing more fully? This question isn't easily answered. Certainly the act of going to one's Center is critical. Such an act is facilitated through meditation and prayer. I do know that my spouse and I still see the world in very different ways. She tends to be aware of where the 't's' need crossing and the 'i's' need dotting. I think I see the larger picture and reflect on ways in which synthesis can occur. I can easily overlook important details.

I know that her sense of order is strong, and when that order is disturbed, she understandably experiences stress. Her need for security is much stronger than mine. Unfortunately, I often contribute to this stress when I am not sensitive to her need for order or don't keep the doors locked when we are in the area.

From another perspective, however, I am well organized. My sense of organization tends to focus on larger tasks rather than on details. For example, in meetings when I sense that a consensus has been reached, but the discussion goes on, I get uneasy and will 'call for the question' so we can move on to the next item.

I also know that I have a much stronger kinesthetic sense than she. For me, the sense of touch influences me profoundly. I can also be deeply touched emotionally and spiritually. When my need for touch has not been met in our relationship, it is easy for me to feel isolated and alone. When I feel touched emotionally or physically, it is easy for me to quickly shift my frame of reference. Feelings of isolation then quickly fade away.

On the other hand, my wife feels isolated and alone when I do not respond to her need for the kind of order and structure that is comfortable for her but often confining to me.

When either of us in some way feels powerless, one of our sub-personalities is likely to take over. Then we can quickly lock into old behaviors. Interestingly enough, such old behaviors had a lot to do with our getting together in the first place.

If my wife plays what I perceive to be a 'mother' role, I quickly rebel. If she perceives the 'dramatist' in me is operating, her 'critic' will point out that I am searching for attention. Then other sub-personalities quickly get into the action. Neither of us is able to be in touch with our respective Centers when such sibling rivalry among our sub-personalities gets activated.

Beginning Again!

Eugene:

In December, 1998, we celebrated fifty years of marriage. For a time, I had considerable discomfort about this approaching date. In part, my discomfort was related to the fear that I would be playing a role that wasn't fully authentic. I was only too aware that there were gaps in our communication.

These fears were largely dissipated. My wife experienced four major surgeries in the months approaching our anniversary. During these crises, there were new expressions of caring for each other. We were both confronted with the fragility of life as well as with our vulnerabilities. While our relationship is less than idyllic, there is a level of playfulness that has been growing. And though not every ambivalent feeling has completed evaporated, the celebration of our fifty years together was truly an exciting event that gave strong affirmation to the commitment that we have made to stay in the relationship.

Time Out for Reflection

Reflect on a time in your life when the process of reconciliation was thwarted before significant changes, in a given relationship, had a chance to occur. (+++) How did you experience the blocks? (+++) Which aspect of your internal self (referred to in this book as sub personalities) took over? (+++) What need was that sub-personality attempting to fill? (+++)

It's Never Too Late

When there is a change of perception that derives from and supports the healing process, that change can result in a new behavior that is nothing short of revolutionary.

Eugene:

Norm was a middle-aged veteran who was a patient in ward, which I directed, in the VA Neuropsychiatric facility for about ten years. He was profoundly depressed and had made several serious suicidal attempts.

Judged to be legally incompetent, he had been legally committed to this institution. His family had not visited him for years. At best, he could be considered to have a dull-normal level of intelligence and certainly was not considered a candidate for discharge in any foreseeable future. In fact, hospital records described him as suffering from deep despair without hope for recovery.

Feeling emotionally shakey, he requested to be placed in a 'locked ward.' I ceeded his request but assured him that he could return to our unit when he felt he was ready. After an extended period of time, Norm eventually requested that he be returned to the open ward which I was supervising. A few weeks later, he asked for a pass because he wanted to apply for a job at the local Post Office. I granted the request and told him to report to me after his interview. I seriously doubted that he would be hired but I suggested that the hiring officials call me at the hospital if they were interested in his candidacy for employment.

To my surprise and chagrin, I received a call from the Post Office officials indicating they were interested in employing Norm. Given the history of his pathology and hospitalization, I panicked. Among other things, I had concerns about whether my colleagues would view my endorsement of Norm's employment outside of the hospital as an incompetent decision.

In my conversation with the Post Office officials, I painted a severe clinical picture and presented Norm's prognosis of success on the job as highly questionable. When they continued to express interest in his employment, I reluctantly agreed to make the necessary arrangements for Norm to get back and forth from the hospital to the Post Office. I instinctively knew that there were no other good options. If I didn't support him in his attempt to work outside the hospital, Norm would lose hope. If he lost hope, he would seriously regress in his behavior and could be doomed to live out his life in the belief that he was unable to function outside a hospital setting.

The only feasible transportation for Norm was to ride a bicycle on a heavily trafficked four lane highway. Since he worked a late shift, he routinely would return to the hospital sometime after midnight. In spite of the many obstacles he had to overcome, he was able to function well in his new work setting. After a trial period of nearly eight months, he was performing well beyond any the expectations I had for him. There was every indication that Norm also was beginning to see himself in a whole new way.

One of my last official acts as I was leaving that setting for new employment was to discharge Norm from the hospital. Given the bureaucratic nature of a government hospital, I was afraid that someone reading his long psychiatric history would be tempted to call him back to the hospital. So I arranged a discharge which would prevent such action. The last report I had about Norm several years later indicated that he was functioning well in his new world.

The processes of grace that lead ultimately to reconciliation always empowers the human spirit. Such empowerment often is manifested in the most unusual and vital ways. Robert Keck, our "evolutionary theologian," notes that change is never fulfilled nor fulfilling without the discovery of personal power and the sharing of that power with the world outside.

Road Signs Along the Way

A damaged self-image can be an impediment to reconciliation. Eugene now recognizes that his early perception of a call to the ordained Christian ministry was somewhat flawed. Circumstances in his early developmental years led him to believe that he was lacking in intellectual abilities and was in many respects a second class citizen. His pattern of academic underachievement in his developmental years created a self-fulfilling prophecy that reinforced these false beliefs which he has held about himself since childhood. The small fundamentalist church of which he was a part placed a great deal of emphasis on the call of God to the Christian ministry. He now realizes that his response to what he perceived as God's call represented a rather desperate effort to validate himself as a person. His attendance at a small, unaccredited, Bible College was a significant turning point in his life. While his earlier patterns of seeing himself as a person of limited abilities continued to persist, these false images were gradually being eroded and replaced with more self-affirming attitudes. His initial assignment to a mission church was a difficult assignment at best. It contained little emotional or financial support.

Eugene:

Six decades ago, I was serving my first congregation as pastor of a struggling church in Columbia, S.C.; no young pastor should have been subjected to the trying conditions that were present. There were only a handful of children, who typically left church after the Sunday School hour. For the few adults who were present, commitment to creating a church community was at best marginal. In fairness, they really provided no opposition, nor did they provide any energy for the church's development.

I was at a loss on how to proceed. I tried calling on the neighbors living the area in an effort to promote the church. Quite honestly, however, there wasn't a great deal to promote. Much of that first year in the pastorate, I was 'at sea'—not knowing what to do next.

A gracious woman, probably in her sixties who lived across the street from the church, became seriously ill. Although she was a member of another denomination, I called on her frequently during her hospital stay. In part, I wanted to show pastoral concern and be a good neighbor to a person who lived close to the church. Beyond that, I was desperately searching for ways to be a pastor.

Over the months, I often went considerably out of my way in an attempt to minister to her. I sensed she had a terminal illness although I had never been told such. While I had no training at that time in how to be helpful to those who were living out their final days, I sensed it was important to assist her in examining her fears regarding her approaching death and to help her draw on her faith resources.

I dealt with this subject cautiously and tentatively—obviously unsure of how to proceed. Her husband, who seemed to be very dependent on her, got very upset. On one occasion, as he was ordering me out of her hospital room, he reminded me that I was not her pastor and had no business being there.

I think this was the most devastating experience of my then twenty-two years on the planet. I left the hospital questioning my adequacy as a minister and felt that I had totally failed. I didn't sleep for several nights. Reliving the scene over and over again, I became essentially dispirited and immobilized. Moreover, I didn't share my feelings of devastation with a single person, not even my wife. Day after day, I tortured myself with internal message that I had failed miserably.

A couple of weeks later the woman died. I wanted so much to offer some evidence of my concern and sense of loss, probably in an attempt to compensate in some way for my perceived inadequacy. I remember going to the funeral home to express my condolences.

It was one of the hardest things I had ever tried to do. My heart was pounding as I approached the entrance to the funeral home. When I discovered that no family member was present at that moment, I was immensely relieved. I signed the guest book that would later be given to the family and then quickly disappeared.

During the next several months, I dreaded the day when I would face this woman's husband. I was convinced he would again be judgmental toward me. I knew, however, that our meeting was inevitable because the front lawns of the church were directly across the street from his home.

In the meantime, I had experienced a great deal of panic about visiting people in the hospital. I feared that I would unknowingly do something that someone would object to or, worse yet, do something that would be seen as painful and damaging.

One day, I discovered what seemed to be a broken underground waterline on the front lawn of the church. There was no money in the church treasury. So, in spite of having no plumbing skills whatsoever, I, along with a helper who happened to be a black laborer, (unthinkable in the early '50s in the south to work side by side with him), began to dig up the church's front yard in an effort to locate the problem.

While I was digging furiously, the neighbor from across the street saw my plight and came over to speak to me. This was our first contact since the night he had ordered me out of his wife's hospital room. I soon recognized his gesture as an apology for his overreaction, and as a desire for reconciliation. Healing occurred for both of us that day.

I didn't have the training or understanding to recognize that his angry, critical response in the hospital that fateful night had to do with his fears about losing his wife on whom he had been so dependent. I wish now that I had been able to recognize those fears for what they were, and had been able to 'hang in there' and help him deal with his panic. As I assess this event many years later, I realize that my intuitions to minister in this way had been essentially accurate, but I didn't have the skills to deal helpfully with his anger and my own panic.

Neither of us knew how to deal directly with the healing and forceful energy of forgiveness and healing. Awkward and as incomplete as it may have been, the process of forgiveness and healing had begun. This experience, so devastating for me in the beginning, has made a major contribution to whatever skills of ministry and counseling that I may have developed.

A Brief Look at an Old Question

Roberto Assagioli's work in Psychosynthesis has been important to us for several reasons. It is one of the earlier attempts to focus in a holistic way on healing. Assagioli anticipated the focus on human potential. Beyond that, he evolved a new way, at least for us, to look at the old philosophical and theological issues relating to questions about the nature of the human condition. Is the human being inherently good or inherently evil? Does mind influence body? (+++) Is health an absence of illness? (+++) How does healing occur? (+++) These questions, in our view, have profound implications for how health, healing, and human potential are approached.

Put in a simple way, if the human species is inherently evil, then how does an inherently evil person do good things? If, on the other hand, humans are inherently good, how can basically good people do alarming and awful things?

Though Assagioli did not deal directly with this philosophical dilemma, it seems to us that he made a significant contribution in moving beyond the debate. He points out that at our Center we are rooted in what he terms universal energy. Furthermore, when we are centered, we recognize that while we have a body, we are more than the body; while we have a mind, we are more than our mind; while we have emotions, we are more than our emotions. At the Center, we are in touch with the image of God within each of us. At the Center, he would insist that we are inherently good. At the Center, we are essentially spirit.

Assagioli notes that we develop aspects of ourselves called sub-personalities, which, in a sense, represent the ways that we both experience and present ourselves in the world. It might be interesting to raise the question about how sub-personalities come to be. Somewhat analogous to biological conception, it occurs to us that our sub-personalities (or behaviors) are influenced through our genetic history as well as through the acculturation process. However this development occurs, the sub-personalties do represent our effort to cope and survive in the world.

As discussed in the opening chapter, Assagioli makes a distinction between the intentions of sub-personalities and the behavioral characteristics of the sub-personalities. He states the intentions of the sub-personalities, which are typically at the edge of or, often, beyond conscious awareness, are always good, primarily because these intentions are energized by a universal energy. The behavioral dimensions of the sub-personality, on the other hand, represent the attempt to accommodate or translate this energy in the every day world. To the degree that intentions become linked with appropriate behavior, to that same degree the sub-personalities will become effective, efficient, and create internal harmony. To the degree that distorted behavior becomes linked with a given intention, to that same degree the sub-personalities will be less effective and distorted.

Eugene:

The following illustrations will illuminate the above concept. Many of my peers grew up in strict fundamentalistic environments emphasizing stringent behavioral prohibitions.

They clearly felt stifled by all the restriction and yearned for ways of expressing their autonomy. Smoking, for example was strictly forbidden. Hence, smoking for them often became a way to break loose from the deadening aspects of a system they experienced as essentially repressive. Smoking also became an attempt to gain peer approval. At the intentions level, one's desire to find autonomy as well as social approval was good and valid.

At the behavior level, however, smoking to gain autonomy and secure friendships is a seriously flawed strategy because it has life threatening consequences. If a person whose original intentions associated with smoking behavior was to gain a measure of autonomy, then strategies designed to carry out these intentions are highly ineffective if the person is still smoking decades later when the original intentions are no longer valid. In such situations, it is likely that the intentions have gone underground and the goal of gaining autonomy is thwarted.

Discovering the intentions of behavior through strategies such as guided meditation becomes a significant tool in facilitating change. Once discovered, we can identify behaviors that more appropriately and efficiently carry out the life affirming intentions.

Taking the Plunge!

The process of healing, which includes confession, repentance, forgiveness of self and others, and reconciliation, begins to take place when we can employ the behavioral strategies that are more in tune with the intentions that come from the Center of one's being.

In recent years, the world has been witness to some astonishing first steps in the journey of reconciliation between cultures. Rabin and Arafat, at the center of the Arab-Israeli drama, had spent most of their adult lives representing their respective cultures, each of which was pledged to destroy the other. It was a transcendent moment when they shook hands and each, in his own words, announced his intentions to give peace a chance. Who can forget former Prime Minister Rabin's words that enough blood had been shed and that it was now time for peace! The political and personal risks that each took were truly astonishing.

In 1977, Prime Minister Rabin was assassinated. A strong representation from the United States was at his funeral. It was deeply moving to hear former enemies, who had been soundly defeated by General Rabin as Israel's Chief of Staff, speak so eloquently. Egypt's President Mubarak, making his first trip to Jerusalem since that defeat, was most impressive. King Hussein of Jordan was passionate in his plea that it was now time to take bold new steps toward the path of reconciliation.

Reconciliation always involves releasing that which is deadening. This typically means that a measure of perceived security needs to be released. Both Mubarak and Hussein movingly articulated that to keep things the way they were could only lead to despair, disillusionment, and barriers that abort the human spirit.

Even though the political environment in that part of the world since those events has been tense and disruptive, it might be argued that the impact of those halting steps toward reconciliation have left a deep imprint on the national psyche of the people of that area.

What Do You Do When You're Stalled?

We have said that the process of confession, repentance, forgiveness, and reconciliation cannot come into being without grace being present. Graceful experiences have a strong element of the miraculous. What occurs when we are not able to fully experience the life changing force of grace? Why do we stay stuck or at best experience only a partial healing? (+++)

Eugene:

This failure to break through the barriers of a relationship can certainly be painful. I am keenly aware of such a failure in my own life. My experience with a person with whom I have experienced a lack of grace vividly points out the complexity of the reconciling process. This particular person has many gifts and talents. He is bright and articulate, and I have often been moved by his ability to be caring. I have also experienced him as highly judgmental and critical. From my perspective, he can be highly rigid and demanding while, at the same time, be generous and giving.

I confess that I have often been immobilized in his presence. In the past, my strong pleaser sub-personality has invested a great deal of energy in winning his approval. As I have experienced our relationship, my attempts to please have only resulted in deep frustration and further immobilization. I have felt judged as incompetent and incapable.

While I have made several attempts to work through these barriers by seeking the guidance of several friends, I confess that I have tended to avoid him, although my avoidance has not been satisfying to me. Even though I no longer am in a position where his approval is important, I confess that, when I have an occasion to discuss our past relationship with trusted friends, I have felt discomfort. My discomfort surely points to unfinished business. My sub-personalities have valiantly tried to resolve the hurt and pain growing out of this conflict, a job which is both inappropriate and impossible for the sub-personalities to accomplish.

It is true that when we see each other, superficial pleasantries are exchanged. I am keenly aware, however, that I have little desire to be in his presence. As I am writing these words I am aware that the subliminal angry feelings that I have been harboring since the demise of our regular contacts dissipated as soon as I owned them.

Why did I tend to avoid him? For one thing, I perceived that I was in a 'no win' situation. There was no grace present. This was easy for me to rationalize by taking note of his history of intense conflicts experienced in other relationships. Still I was 'copping-out.' Even if there were no foreseeable way to win, that fact really didn't let me 'off the hook.' My pleaser dictated that, as a pastor, I should keep the stress, which was growing out of confrontation, to a minimum. My pleaser had no tools with which to win, and I could conceive of no way to bring about reconciliation. I was not `in tune' with my integrative Center. Is this pattern any different than those involving ongoing, unresolved conflicts on an international scale?

Why did I still hang onto unresolved feelings when I spoke of him? Is my scorekeeper trying to protect me from my pleaser? Am I still the 'hurt child' that, very early in life, learned not to confront authority? Is my pleaser inundated with a sense of failure?

In the language of Psychosynthesis, one role of the integrative Center is to give coordination to our sub-personalities. A significant function in this coordinating activity is to recognize the intentions of the behaviors of these sub-personalities. In this case, the pleaser's intention might be to avoid strife and conflict. The workaholic sub-personality may be intending to gain approval through strenuous activity. The behavior of sub-personalities may indeed be inappropriate while the intention of the behavior is to tap into the God-like qualities of the Center which is in tune with the higher universal energies.

Although my sub-personalities are still trying to resolve the hurt and pain that grew out of the conflict described earlier, that is a job which is both inappropriate and impossible for sub-personalities to accomplish. That resolution must come from my Center—the source of healing.

While it would be helpful if the other person had also been seeking resolution to the situation I've described, it isn't necessary. Reconciliation is ultimately an 'inside job.' Resolution for me can be achieved unilaterally by spending time in meditation and prayer. Part of the overall resolution is to love and accept my sub-personalities which valiantly do the best they know how, although they are often ineffective in their attempt to deal with conflict. Alignment with the positive intentions of a given sub-personality is a critically important basic step toward reconciliation and healing.

Earlier we stated that our "internal children" sub-personalities play a valuable role in our lives but are not part of the Center of our lives. Just as our biological children come from us but are not us, so our sub-personalities come from us but are not us. Like children, sub-personalities can feel responsible for tasks for which they have no responsibility. For example, consider a seven-year-old child who gets the idea that her family is facing a financial crisis. She may assume that it is her task to solve this crisis. As a result, she may try to figure how to make her allowance stretch in order to make the house payments. Soon, of course, this child will feel overwhelmed, trying to make the house payment with her meager allowance. Once the parents become aware of the child's intentions, they may express their gratitude for the child's sensitivity while assuring her that the house payment isn't her responsibility. The parents, however, may assign an age-appropriate task to the child that affirms her desire to play a responsible role in the way the family functions. Similarly, when we are centered, it is possible to express appreciation for the behavioral intentions of our sub-personalities.

When Things Change!

How can healing and reconciliation occur for persons who have made a decision to leave a marriage? Often each person has experienced so much hurt and anger that each is tempted to forfeit positive experiences that they have shared. Rarely is there a conscious effort by couples leaving a marriage to negotiate a "new" relationship with each other. Such a "new" relationship could lead them to respect the history that they have shared together—a history that could be preserved even though the marriage relationship is dissolved. Reconciliation can indeed take place even though the couple may choose to go their respective ways.

The process of releasing hurts and expectations is an important dimension of the process of reconciliation. In our view, this applies when couples are changing the status of their relationships. When one person in a relationship has made the decision to leave, the other person has no functional alternative but to release the one who wants to leave. For the person who wants the marriage to survive, releasing the spouse is especially painful and difficult. At this point, the person wanting the marriage to survive can get caught in behaviors that are highly self-defeating. Even if the person who wants desperately to hang on to the marriage is successful in convincing her/his spouse to stay in the marriage against that partner's better judgment, that victory will be hollow at best.

Eugene:

Following active military duty, a friend and I had one of the most exciting and stimulating experiences of our lives. We became 'bush pilots' in the South American jungles and contacted Amer-Indians who had had no previous contact with the 'outside' world. It was a period of our lives when we took enormous risks and engaged in adventures which had no right to succeed.

My friend and I were the first contacts that they had seen from the 'outside world' and hence. (One small band of hunters did report that they had seen a small group of people who were descendents of African slaves, but had reported that this band of people had quickly faded away.)

These Indians had a unique way of relating to visitors. When strangers visit the tribe, tribal members take distinctive action to determine ways to relate to the newcomers. Shortly after meeting a stranger, the Trio Indian will engage the newcomer in an extended conversation and negotiation. The basic question is: What way do we relate to each other? What roles are to be played out in the relationship?

For example, if an older male meets a younger man, their discussion may start with the possibility of them relating as father and son. If both agree that such is a viable relationship, then each respectively accepts the responsibilities that are implicit with the role of father and son. If such roles seem ill-fitting, they may choose to be uncle and nephew to each other. While that relationship is more distant than father/son, it still carries certain responsibilities with it. It is also possible to choose a still more distant relationship, such as distant cousins.

If a man meets a woman, they may agree to be brother and sister. If this agreement is made it is understood that this will not be a sexual relationship since a sexual relationship is totally inappropriate for brothers and sisters. They may also choose a more distant relationship such as cousins. Regardless, each relationship carries with it certain responsibilities to be played out. The important principle with this culture is that people, including strangers, are accepted as family members in some way.

A creative aspect of such negotiated relationship options are that individuals who discover that a given relationship pattern is no longer viable for them have the potential to re-negotiate a new relationship, assuming a different role.

Looking at Divorce Differently

Eugene, continuing:

Some years after finishing my doctoral studies, it occurred to me that the relational patterns of the Trio Indians might have implications for our cultural ideas about divorce. I became convinced that there had to be alternatives to the destructive and negative experiences that divorce often produces.

Borrowing from the Trio Indian tradition of negotiating family or extended family relationships, it occurred to me that couples in the process of divorce could negotiate a kind of new relationship that would not cut each other out of family and extended relational patterns. Rather than thinking of divorce as a rupturing end of a relationship, it might be thought of as an opportunity for negotiating the beginning of a new relationship offering distinctly different ways of relating.

I reasoned that before a couple reached the place where they could generate no alternatives but to destroy each other within the marriage, they would be better served to negotiate a new relational contract. When I would counsel with couples who had announced plans for a divorce, my typical comment was something like, 'Congratulations, you have made an important decision. But you're only half way there. How are you going to love each other now that you have decided not to continue being husband and wife?'

Many couples have commented that they learned how to be friends once they had been divorced. They had obviously taken important steps in learning how to care about each other in a more creative way. Still, there may be another important step. They may develop ways to be intentionally included in each other's families. For example, they could choose to relate to each as brother and sister or, if more emotional space was needed, they could choose to relate to each other as cousins. Choosing alternative ways of relating to each other could have important social implications.

After appropriate therapeutic work has been completed, former spouses could actively participate in family festivals and celebrations such as graduations, weddings and other important events as family members. Troubled husbands and wives need to find ways to recreate their love that would be both healing and enriching to their relationship's bottom line, namely reconciliation.

Choosing Life

In the beginning of this book we suggested that healing is a matter of one becoming a whole person—indeed, a holistic experience involving the gamut of human experience (physical, emotional, spiritual, social, and intellectual). Dr Donald Tubesing, a former director of a holistic wellness center we have referred to earlier, has suggested that symptoms of behavioral problems impact all these areas of our lives. Furthermore, there is abundant literature pointing to the connections among the physical, emotional, spiritual, social and intellectual realms of our experience. While the exact nature of these interactions and relationship patterns is still a mystery, there is little doubt that strong interactions and patterns exist.

It is important to be pro-active in making these holistic kinds of connections. In some ways we are continually making choices between life and death. As we experience the processes of confession, repentance, forgiveness and reconciliation, we choose life. This choice is of course risky. But what do we have to lose other than our fears, insecurities and barriers that don't serve us well in the first place?

Eugene:

Sally, a nurse, was one of the first persons who became my client when I started my private practice of Psychology in Tucson. She stated that she was at 'loose ends' with her life and lack of direction and purpose. Sensing that she was experiencing and existential crisis, I began inquiring about her religious commitments. She responded that she had only been in church on three occasions: A wedding and two funerals. She added, almost in a coincidental way, that she hadn't been feeling well but thought that she may be experiencing psychosomatic symptoms.

A new Bible-study group had just been organized by nearly twenty physicians and their wives, as well as Leta and myself, who wanted to seriously explore the spiritual dimensions in their lives as well as how they could apply these discoveries to their personal and professional lives. When I described this group to Sally, she was eager to join in these kinds of discussions.

Because of her background, her questions and comments were more basic and elementary, while on the other hand, most of the physicians had a significant involvement in religious discussions. Many were attempting to find a more creative and meaningful way to make their faith commitment more relevant. In the first meetings in which Sally was involved, I wasn't at all sure she was going to be a 'good fit' for the group.

In the meantime Sally, then thirty-nine years old, learned that she had a rare disease that had only affected a small group of women and no men. In every case, the disease had become quickly fatal for these women. It became very clear that Sally's days were numbered.

Shortly after discovering that she had this disease, she told the group that she had heard about the, 'laying on of hands,' adding that she had no idea of what it was but asked these physicians and their wives if they would, 'do this for her.' Everyone panicked, including me. When she realized that everyone had become immobilized by her question, her eyes darted between one person and then another. Her question was: 'Did I say something wrong?'

A female psychician, who was part of the Jewish tradition, had come by to check out this group. When she saw Sally's anquish, she raced across the room and threw her arms around Sally saying, 'I don't know what it is either, but let's do it.' We all collected our emotional and spiritual balance, gathered around Sally, and did indeed lay our hands on her as we prayed together.

The moments that followed were powerful, graceful, and profoundly healing for all of us. In many ways Sally, who had been considered naive by some of the group members, became our teacher on how to live and how to die.

As her disability become more incapacitating, she was unable to attend our lively weekly meetings. Just weeks before her passing, Sally asked me to check with the group to see if they would meet in her bedroom where she was now confined. The group quickly consented, although it was clear that they were feeling very awkward and unsure of what to say.

The different members made casual comments about the University of Arizona Wildcats as well as a sundry of other topics. Finally, my discomfort level became so high that I had to speak.

'Sally,' I began, 'it looks like you won't be with us much longer. I want you to know how much I love you and how much you have impacted my life.'

The ice broke and there was an outpouring of love from us to her and her to us. When it came time to say goodbye, Sally offered a moving benediciton for all of us. That moment will forever be etched in our hearts and minds.

Sally's memorial service was held on the Saturday before Easter Sunday—the day that would have been her fortieth birthday. She had planned her memorial service as a celebration. She had requested that we all be present and asked that we share something about the life-changing and grace-filled moments that we had all experienced together.

Sally had come to us wanting to be a learner. However, she, like the rest of us, became both teacher and learner. Something beautiful happened through Sally's group involvement—something that approached love without conditions.

At the beginning of our spiritual journey together, none of us anticipated the significance of our encounters or the power of change that would occur within us. Often the gifts of grace come in a least expected way and catch us by surprise. When this occurs, we find new strength for the journey.

Speaking of this journey and the strength that we need for it, someone has observed the following: 'God offers minimum security but maximum support' as we move out of the perceived safety zone and choose the risky business of being alive.

A Time for Reflection

Reflect on a time when a difficult problem had been solved, or there was healing in a non-nurturing relationship; or a time when everything seemed back 'on track,' when the energy once present, then cut off, was returned and enriched. (+++)

How was grace/unconditioned acceptance experienced? (+++) Were you aware of how that was initiated? (+++) And how you felt about it? (+++)

How was the confession or ownership carried out? (+++) Were all persons involved free to share how the disruption affected them? (+++) Were you aware of the moment you wished to change or when the other person was willing to change? (+++) How did you experience the process emotionally, physically, spiritually, intellectually and socially? (+++) What began to happen in the relationship that informed you that forgiveness was beginning to take place? (+++) How was grace/unconditional acceptance experienced? (+++) Were you aware of how this was initiated? How you felt about it? (+++)

Chapter 7
Facing the Future

An Epoch Size Change Is In The Works!

Even though God has planted eternity in the hearts of human kind,even so, we cannot grasp the full scope of God's works from beginning to end. **Ecclesiastes 3:11**

I'm free,
I'm free to be kind to all I meet
Do good wherever I can,
Help my brother, sisters make a plan
That brings us peace and joy.

I'm free,
I'm free to go throughout our mighty land,
Where I can take a stand
Against the rebel band
that kills equality.

I'm free
I'm free to be me.
[Carroll Rinehart]

THERE ARE MANY PEOPLE warning about the survival of our planet. Pollutants are threatening the water that we drink and the air that we breathe, apparently at a rate never before experienced in history. The polar ice capes are melting and global warming, with potential changes in the environment, may threaten life as we know it. Enormous gaps exist between cultures and economic groups. There are shocking rates of violence and, according to most commentators, the use of illegal drugs has reached epidemic proportions. Many nations, including increasing numbers of third-world nations, have nuclear capabilities that could seriously threaten existence on our fragile planet. Are we facing the beginning of the end, or are there signs of hope in the midst of this potential chaos?

It is said that the Chinese character for crisis has two meanings. One meaning is danger; the other is opportunity. Philosophers and theologians for centuries have maintained that we are made in the image of God. While this concept may be difficult to define and demonstrate in scientific terms, it is in basic agreement with the philosophy of Psychosynthesis that has been a keystone to the thesis of this book.

We do hold an optimistic view of the resiliency of the human spirit. While the dangers of extinction are very real, we are in accord with those who believe we are on the brink of new ways of thinking and being.

There is a wonderful story told in the delightful book, *Chicken Soup for the Soul: 101 Stories to Open the Heart and Rekindle the Spirit*, by Canfield & Hansen, entitled The Golden Buddha.(28) It's the deeply moving narrative of a clay image of Buddha that was being moved in 1957 as a result of highway construction in the rapidly growing city of Bangkok, Thailand. As the crane was lifting the Buddha, the clay began to crack because of its weight. Since it was raining, the head monk decided to abandon the move for the time being and leave the Buddha image in its place until after the rain. During the night, this monk returned to the site to see if the Buddha was protected from the rain. When he lifted the tarp and shined his flashlight on the image, he spotted something very unusual. The light of his flashlight reflected back a sliver of golden light.

With excitement, the monk ran to the monastery and quickly returned with hammer and chisel. To his astonishment, as he chipped away the clay, there was a thirty feet tall Buddha image of solid gold, valued at over 200 million dollars at the time this discovery was made.

Historians surmised that when the Burmese army was about to invade Thailand several hundred years ago, the monks, realizing that the solid gold image would be confiscated, decided to cover the image with clay and thus disguise its value. After all, who would want to steal a simple clay image? It appears that the Burmese slaughtered all the monks, and the secret of this extraordinary solid gold Buddha remained intact until that fateful day in 1957.

While this amazing story has historical truth, it is also a powerful metaphor. Often hidden under the hard protective crust of our collective and individual developmental histories are immense possibilities. Even cultures, which in the past have made amazing contributions to the evolution of human kind, have gone through periods of self-destruction. When one studies the Greek and Roman cultures, to appreciate their historical developments and contributions, one wonders whether their respective decline and eventual destruction were inevitable. Is there a parallel in the aging process that each of us experiences? Is the process of decay the fate of every civilization, including the cultures of both East and West? Where are the seeds of destruction and decay? Are there other choices that cultures such as ours might make that would be more life-enhancing?

We might raise the question, what causes this death and decay? In the dynamic beginnings of a creative force, there is a clear sense of mission and purpose. However, the focus of this creative beginning soon shifts to preservation and protection. Institutional walls are erected. Soon the dynamic force, almost imperceptibly at first, begins to ebb away.

If one looks at the decline and demise of the Greek and Roman cultures, do we find some underlying principle equivalent to the encrusting of the golden Buddha? Does the "golden Buddha" still lie beneath the crust that awaits a resurrection? In the midst of ruin and decay, is it possible that something enduring will remain?

As we look at our own culture in which violence has taken on epidemic proportions, and the gap between the have's and have not's continues to grow, are we going down the same road our Greek and Roman ancestors traveled? Is there hope for us and our society? Perhaps our salvation from ourselves lies in seizing the meaning of the promise of that metaphorical golden Buddha.

When people are excluded either by age, class, race, culture or geography, the golden Buddha will indeed remain hidden. When bold new steps are taken to be inclusive by creating opportunities for those who live below the poverty line then slivers of light may emerge in the clay that hides the golden Buddha. When children whose living conditions are impoverished have an opportunity to see themselves and their potential in new light, pieces of clay that hides a rich treasure will begin to disintegrate. When we begin to cherish our environment by limiting our excessive dependence on material goods, then the hidden glow of the golden Buddha may begin to re-appear.

If we hold to the notion that we are in some unexplainable way made in the image of God, we can be assured that there is something indestructible in our human spirit. We might further conclude that the ideals underlying the democratic principles which inspired our founding fathers can also survive the chaos and apparent decline of our society. If so, then we have solid grounds for optimism about what will eventually be.

Eugene, with four colleagues, concluded a Rotary-sponsored study exchange (GSE) to northern Thailand in 1995. He heard Mr. Jiichiro "Frank" Nakajima, one of the International Trustees and a personal representative of Rotary's International President, make an insightful comment about the stability of his Japanese culture at this point in time. Citing the recent subway gas attacks, he noted that Japanese culture was at that time highly unstable. Mr. Nakajima's challenge to the Rotarians of his country was to embody the ideals of the Rotary motto by putting service above self and thus rediscover, metaphorically speaking, the golden Buddha beneath the encrusted clay. He emphasized that this model of service could be a stabilizing force in a culture that was experiencing a profound crisis.

In a report to Rotary International about this recent GSE experience, Eugene noted that the Rotarians in Thailand and the United States are the power brokers of our respective communities. In both countries the gap between the "have's and have not's" is clearly widening and the economic middle class is steadily shrinking. While the Thai Rotarians are more clearly identified with the wealthy class when compared to the Rotarians in North America, both groups are among the most influential people in their respective societies. The challenge is for influential business professionals to step away from their profit orientation to live out, in a disciplined way, the Rotary motto of truly placing service above self.

It can be argued that the violence of the dog-eat-dog mentality in the business and professional community, as well in the political sphere of action, might indeed fuel some of the violence typically acted out in physical and social ways. Is the violence of gangs and the drug culture different in principle from a businessman who takes unethical shortcuts in an attempt to be the first with the most? What about the politician who puts his/her own selfish self-interest above the common good?

Do we have cause for optimism in the serious disruptions that the cultures of the world seem to be facing? Yes, we can believe in our children who, even in depressive living environments, manage against all odds to make outstanding contributions to their communities and their world.

Eleanor Roosevelt was an extraordinary woman. In the preface of his book entitled, *The Eleanor Roosevelt Story*, Archibald MacLeish states that she suffered through her youth, although she was in an affluent family environment. She was not the beauty that her mother's family was expected to produce, and she lacked the social graces of the young girls of her class. Moreover she was under the tutelage of a grandmother who purportedly didn't approve of her.

It is reported that she spent her early years wanting desperately to be loved, attempting to gain the approval of her social class, but she was largely unsuccessful. In some ways she was like a sleeping beauty waiting for the "kiss of life."(29)

One might raise the question why she, and others like her, managed to surmount the awesome developmental hurdles that could have stunted her emotional and spiritual growth while others have found similar hurdles a prison from which they do not escape.

Equally puzzling is the question why others who have known an enriched environment, with every apparent opportunity to develop their potential, remain blocked and unfilled. Said another way, why is it that some manage to get past the hardened clay to find the "golden Buddha" while others will not? Perhaps we will never know. In our view, it is important that we not forget to remember that this potential is a hallmark and at the very core of the human spirit

Carroll:

A class of seven year-old second graders accepted the invitation to create its own opera. This involved choosing a story, writing the libretto or script, composing the music, casting the parts, staging and performing the final work. This process which took several months culminated in a forty-five minute presentation.

The students chose as their story 'Charlotte's Web' by E. B. White as the basic story for their work. The story is of a runt pig that is saved by a compassionate little girl, Fern. Later, when the pig, Wilbur, becomes too big, he is moved to Uncle Homer Zuckerman's farm. There he meets a new friend, Charlotte, a spider, who by spinning messages in her web helps save Wilbur and gives him prominence.

In the course of events, Wilbur is taken to the fair where he wins prizes. Charlotte accompanies him. As they prepare to return to the farm, Charlotte tells Wilbur she will not be going back because she is about to die.

At this point in the story, the students stalled the process. For three weeks they found a myriad of reasons for not facing Charlotte's impending death. At last we confronted the issue. Reluctantly they began

to talk about Charlotte's death. Suddenly, one child began sobbing. Her teacher invited her to sit next to him, and asked what was wrong. 'I don't want Charlotte to die,' she wept.

What followed was a discussion of death and dying. Then the students created the necessary dialogue to advance the story. That day's writing ended with a question from Wilbur to Charlotte. 'Why do you have to die?' The students were then instructed to go home and think about what might be Charlotte's answer to Wilbur; then write it down and bring it the following day to be shared.

The next morning we gathered in a circle to share the homework writing. Many insightful responses were offered. Then one of the students, Derek, read his version of Charlotte's reply:

'Wilbur, just as summers come and go
So must I.
We have had our time together
And the memories will last a lifetime.
Even though my days are numbered
Yours will be long and happy.
I'll always love you Wilbur.'

Everyone in the circle sat in silent awe, tears welling up in our eyes and trickling down our cheeks. I turned to Derek, not believing that a seven year old could write with such sensitivity and depth of understanding, and asked, 'Derek, how did you do that?'

He replied very simply, 'I was in my room, all alone. I was thinking about Charlotte's answer. All of a sudden the words began coming. I grabbed a sheet of paper and a pencil and wrote them down, crying as I wrote!'

The Dance with Our Mortality and Our Immorality

The stories that we have shared seem, to us, to point to the importance of balancing our understanding of mortality and immortality. From our experience, we know that children develop an awareness of their mortality at an early age. Apparently, humans are the only animals to have this awareness with such acuteness and at such an early developmental age.

Awareness of our mortality often has the tragic implication of causing people to strive excessively for material and physical security, as well as for power and control. Such striving can be interpreted as attempts to push back the limits that mortality imposes.

An unhealthy focus on immortality, on the other hand, may result in such an "other worldly" orientation that one can lack grounding in the here and now. A folksy way of making this observation might go something like "he is so heavenly minded that he is of no earthly good." Clearly, a healthy human orientation lies in creating a balance between mortal and immortal preoccupations. Such a balance is freeing. It not only encourages a person to be 'present' and embrace the here and now, contributing to both the nourishment of the environment and of the human spirit, but also gives one permission to let go of that which must, ultimately, be left behind.

Eugene:

The Reverend Bill Opitz provided an inspiring example for many as he confronted his own mortality/immortality. Although he had never smoked, he was to die of lung cancer, a probable result of inhaling second hand smoke over the years.

My office was located in the same hospital where Bill was to live his final days. I often dropped by to see him while I was seeing other hospitalized patients. On this specific day, Bill had slipped into a mild coma. I sensed that he would be crossing the lines of worlds very soon. I held his hand and shared these words with him: 'Bill, you are very near to the crossing. God go with you.' Within the hour he had breathed his last.

I went to his memorial service. As I might have guessed, he had planned much of the service to be a celebration of life. He had made an audio tape in which he expressed his love for the congregation and thanked them for the generous way they had ministered to him as he also had attempted to minister to them. He spoke with warmth and much love, and told them how important they had been to him. After speaking for awhile, he stated that he had better be going, stating that members of the congregations would be joining him before very long.

What he said next was electrifying. Calling the organist by name, he said, 'Patty, hit that Hallelujah Chorus!' Hit those notes she did. The audience was on their feet, singing at the tops of their voices, celebrating a life with tears of joy.

Our stories have been chosen in an effort to find hope when there appears to be little rationale for hope. The marvelous story of the seven-year-old student named Derek, shared above, was clearly inspired by his involvement with his classmates and with Carroll as, together, they confronted the dilemma posed by the death of Charlotte, the spider.

What will Survive?

The heart of the concept of immortality is rooted in the notions that we are made in the image of God, and that all of life and all of creation are sacred. Central to this concept is the confidence that in the midst of decay and ruin, and in chaos and destruction, all is not lost. Whether it be the continuing contributions of the Greeks, Romans, Egyptians, Aztecs or other great civilizations, all were rooted in beliefs regarding universal and eternal qualities such as love, beauty, truth, justice, faith and wholeness. It is these eternal verities that survive that which is mortal.

Earlier we referred to Robert Keck's notion of three Epochs that have been present in the development of the universe. In the first Epoch, during which humans first made their appearance, there was a sense of cooperation and rhythm between animals and nature.

The second Epoch was characterized by humankind's attempt to control human nature that might be seen as comparable to adolescence. You will remember that he saw this period as a necessary and important aspect of development. Keck regards humankind as being, now, at the end of the adolescent stage. He notes that the authority struggles associated with this stage often result in rebellion and violence in societies, representing societal attempts to develop an identity that will be needed in the next Epoch. This is a crucial and critical developmental stage, one which is two-edged, having enormous potential as well as considerable danger. Characteristics of this adolescent stage include the attempt to draw clear lines between the sacred and secular, matter and spirit, good and evil, and between the individual body, mind, and spirit-dimensions of human existence.

In what Keck calls the dark night of the soul, we begin to see serious defects in the adolescent way of thinking and acting.

"Because of the adolescent's ego's need to be higher than, better than, and on top of the separated other, earthquakes taking place across the human landscapes resulted in one turf being placed on top of another turf. Heaven was seen as higher than earth, divine as higher than human, spirit (until we ignored it altogether) higher than matter, humans higher than the earth or the animals, man higher than woman, and our religion or nation closer to God than others."(30)

To this list, Keck adds the false dichotomy of separating illness from wellness. In attempts to isolate single causes of disease, and to almost exclusively focus on single diseased parts of the person, we have lost something distinctly true about the human being. We are more than our bodies.

In discussing Epoch III, he underlines the interactions of body, mind, spirit and environment in creating states of health and illness. He makes this astute observation: "In our holistic universe everything is interrelated, including our unconscious and our body, as well as our unconscious and the world. In this transitional time, in the move from reductionism to holism, we can only begin to imagine how thoroughly our inner life is manifest in our physical and circumstantial "fate."(31)

Central to Keck's discussion is his observation that love is at the very core and essence of life. Love is fundamental to everything that is. He notes that when and if we move into Epoch III, spiritual maturity will open our eyes to the profoundly essential quality of love that permeates the universe. The challenge, he adds, will be for us to think in new and more mature ways about love.

"Love is the cosmic quality of the Spirit that makes this a holistic universe. Everything is connected precisely because everything has the allurement of love as its most fundamental energy. And this is why our adolescent ego needs to separate things that have been, in one sense, unnatural and responsible for illusions, deceptions, fractures in the collective body, and faults along the human landscape."(32)

Keck offers this important word about the developmental process: "Collectively we are not the 'adult children' of abusive parents. The abuses and illusions from which we suffer are the result of our natural ego development as we grew through adolescence. That makes it a very different picture regarding our future. We fell from the grace of love, not as abused children but as 'prodigal sons'—rebellious adolescents reaching for independence. But the ontological grace and love that we experienced in our childhood is still there in our depths. For a healthy maturity we need only to tap back into our collective soul, find that ontological love that our cosmic 'parents' ordained us with from the very beginning, and grow on into a healthy, whole and holy future. That is part of the reason why the major agenda of our adulthood is spiritual development—rediscovering the love in our souls. As prodigal sons we need only return 'home' to the realization that love has been in us from the very beginning."(33)

What are the maturational signposts that will indicate that we are approaching the healthy maturity that Keck describes? Certainly one such sign will be reflected in a move away from exploitation. Reduced possessiveness, in various forms, would also seem to suggest movement toward maturity. (We wonder if the hostile takeover mentality of big business might imply unresolved emotional conflicts and immaturity associated with the adolescent phase of development?) Surely, motivation would encourage individuals to assume ownership of responsibility for themselves and their actions. Such would preclude commonly heard denials from public political figures caught with their hands in the cookie jar—"I didn't do anything illegal."

Another important landmark of maturity is the presence of an inspiriting dynamic that brings a life-giving quality. It also produces a level of intimacy that gives us freedom to experience a high level of vulnerability.

Keck, in his book entitled, *Sacred Quest: The Evolution and Future of the Human Soul,* makes this observation: "Wholeness does not mean that everything is homogenized into bland soup of sameness. Rather as we leave our adolescent epoch's ego insecurities and grow into adult maturity, we will be able to appreciate the benefits of diversity, each part enriched even further by participation in the whole." He makes reference in this passage to Emmauel Swedenborg, who describes this diversity within wholeness as 'distinguishable oneness.'"

Keck adds that the fault of reductionism was based on the obsession with the part rather than with the whole, but adds that it is important to understand this focus of Epoch II as part of the maturational process, necessary in the entire evolutionary history of the human species. He observes that, "we do not have to demean one particular step in order to take the next step. We would not even be ready for the next step, were it not for the previous one."(34)

Eugene:

Several years ago, I was invited by a good Mexican friend to attend his graduation ceremonies from a medical school in Mexico City. This educational institution is a Roman Catholic University, so it was predictable that a Roman Catholic Mass would precede the actual ceremony. The priest who gave the homily was a distinguished looking older man who gave a marvelous message using the parable of the Good Samaritan. He urged the new doctors to practice from a service orientation, rather than a materialistic focus. To illustrate the point, he spoke of a physician who was an acquaintance of his who owned five expensive cars, summarizing his remarks with the comment: 'What's the point?' When he finished the mass, the new physicians warmly applauded him. I was pleasantly surprised.

I soon learned the reason for their applause. This priest was a trained physician and professor on the medical school staff. All of the graduates had been his students. Furthermore, I learned that he had pancreatic cancer and had only a short time to live. I then realized that he was not only giving his final address to the graduates, but to his colleagues on the Medical School faculty as well. His message had been upbeat and deeply rooted in his faith. I suddenly understood his warm smile and the wave of his hand to his students as he acknowledged their applause and left the stage.

He had first hand knowledge of both his mortality and his immortality. He also clearly knew what truly transcends the transient stage of mortality, and what bears fruit in eternity.

Stand Back for a Better Look

Psychosynthesis, in dealing with changes in human behavior, often involves the process sometimes called dis-association. It is a means of stepping back psychologically to gain a larger perspective and to separate the experience (I) from the experience (it).

Carroll:

When our son was in elementary school, he was assigned to a class with, supposedly, a very strong teacher. It was soon apparent that the class was not a very creative environment and left much to be desired. When visitors were expected, our son knew he would be called upon to produce something that would make the room 'look good.'

This became the topic of conversation at dinner one evening. We explained to him that school is like a game which is played with prescribed rules. Even though moving beyond the rules is where one's greatest potential can often be realized, it remains true that playing outside the rules causes problems for all concerned. In the face of this, however, it is important, while playing the game, to be able to step outside and observe how the game is being played. When one gains a larger perspective and disassociates, while 'playing the game,' it is as important as moving beyond the rules.

Subsequent dinner-time discussions no longer dealt with trite questions such as, 'What happened in school today?' Rather, it was,

'How was the game played today?' The purpose of such questions was to empower our son and to help him give a greater focus to his experience.

The Bottom Line

What have grace, confession, repentance, forgiveness and reconciliation to do with facing the future? The desire to experience the energies and life-giving forces of the universe, through what is referred to in Psychosynthesis as "life qualities" such as love, truth, beauty, justice, faith, joy and wholeness, cannot be legislatively achieved. Furthermore, they are not available to us on demand nor, for that matter, are they endowed. They can only be known through personal choice. One must choose to be "present" to them. This kind of choosing is dramatically illustrated by those individuals who live under desperate conditions and are still able to rise above these conditions and make significant contributions to their society!

Carroll:

I recently met a most amazing person. Born black, out of wedlock, in a ghetto, he has nevertheless been a rising star in the world of conducting. In talking about his beginnings, and his many childhood playmates who 'didn't make it,; I asked him how he was able to make such progress.

'I was lucky,' he said. 'In my schools, I never had a teacher who said, 'You can't because you're black and live in a ghetto.' It was always, 'Of course you can.' My teachers made a difference.

He knew love very early. He experienced grace through unconditional acceptance. He is not afraid to own who he is (confession), knowing that, even though black and growing up in a ghetto, he is much more than that. He knows what he wants for himself, his family and those whose lives he touches. He wills himself to his dream (repentance). His openness to who he is invites others into his dream (forgiveness). As a result, he is effective in his relationships with others, and, he is an exciting role model.

No Choice but to Choose!

We make the choices with whom we engage in life's experiences. We decide if we accept or reject others. If we experience a relationship, job or activity as toxic, we have the option of helping to change the nature of the relationship and our involvement in it. There is no law in the land that can require us to take ownership of our feelings, values, or causes of our joys and despair; such ownership is a very personal matter. If something in me is keeping me from becoming more of what I'd like to be, only I can own it fully, and, in owning it, be able to let it go. Each of us holds the keys to confession and to the main entrance which give access to the life-giving forces.

If we fully own what is, and are willing to change, we are empowered to begin the change process. But the will to change, to experience a fuller, more meaningful life, is a choice we must make individually. What we value, how we view meaning in life must become a part of this choice. If we place misguided value on power, and if we believe our mortality is connected to that power, then repentance is compromised. It is common for our adolescent culture to believe that control and/or wealth are the essence of power. Isn't it strange that Christ's power was not in wealth and control but in empowering the individual! He didn't order the lame to walk but offered that possibility, "If you want to be whole, pick up your bed and walk." The individual must want to take action.

Forgiveness, A Powerful Force

Forgiveness is another human experience that cannot be legislated or demanded, even though, as children, we are often admonished and told, "Say you're sorry!" How difficult it can be to say one is sorry and mean it in a heartfelt way. For some, it's an easy cliché to get others to lower their expectations. Yet, when forgiveness is truly authentic, it is indeed a powerful experience.

A story of forgiveness, having its origins during the Japanese occupation of Thailand, was brought to a happy closure in 1993.

Eric Lomax was a British soldier. Captured by the Japanese during

WWII, he was tortured and, with hundreds of other prisoners of war, forced to build the "Death Railway" on which the famed River Kwai bridge became so well known. It was there that approximately 100,000 Asian slave laborers and 16,000 Allied prisoners died of disease or by execution.

An interpreter, Takashi Nagasi, who served with the Japanese military policemen, has returned to this site often in his quest for personal atonement. He also saw this quest as having implications for what he referred to as atonement for his nation. He tracked down many of the prisoners and gave them support and spoke of reconciliation.

Eric Lomax, haunted by his memories, sought resolution or even revenge for the terrible suffering he had endured as a POW. At age seventy-five, he finally came face-to-face with Nagasi. Instead of expressing hatred, the two men grasped hands and shed tears. Nagasi apologized for what the Japanese had done during the War. Although branded a traitor by many Japanese, he continued to beg forgiveness of former Allied prisoners. (35)

When grace, confession, repentance and forgiveness are experienced, then reconciliation may occur. It is then that we are able to rise to a higher level of awareness, sensitivity and responsiveness—states of being that are precursors to Keck's Epoch III.

Can hope exist in a society that has little trust in its political leaders? Can hope exist when justice becomes a legal game played out by lawyers within the 'justice' system? Can hope exist when education is curtailed from providing those experiences that cultivate the core of human-ness and then ask educators to solve social inequities, as well as meet the needs of government and industry? Can hope exist when our values have become so skewed by the glamorization of violence and avarice, and when strength is viewed as one's ability to overpower another?

A community, church, school, neighborhood, city, country cannot function to its fullest potential if the individual is not empowered. Christ sought to provide humankind with a means to individual empowerment. Love was central to that means. Love, experienced as an invitation to join the flow of energy in the universe, is the answer. Yes, hope can exist in all the situations described above where the golden Buddha of love abides at the core.

An Invitation to Be

Numerous times we have referred to Psychosynthesis and its emphasis on our Center as the core of our being. In this chapter we have focused on facing the future. From this perspective, our major responsibility is to learn to invite others into experiencing this Center, encouraging each other to make the life-enhancing choices that make a true difference in lives. We need to align with, and become a part of, the energies of the universe, and in so doing transform and release those same energies in others and into the things we create.

We must decide what is truly important in this human endeavor. We must know how to live in balance with our mortality and our immortality. That which transcends our temporary, mortal needs becomes part of our immortality.

A Time To Reflect

Think for a few moments about your responses to ideas presented in the previous chapters. What were some of the moments in your life when you were keenly aware of grace, confession, repentance, forgiveness and reconciliation? (+++) What feelings were present in those moments? How did you experience a sense of wholeness within yourself as you moved through each step? (+++)

How much vulnerability did you experience? (+++) How scary or risky was it for you to take yourself onward? (+++) And how significant were the issues that came to mind in your life and relationships? (+++) Are you now at peace with them? (+++) And how did you bring about resolution for yourself? (+++)

Make a list of things that energize you and leave you with a sense of inspiritedness. (+++) Reflect on your relationships in terms of the presence of grace/unconditional acceptance, confessions of owning what is, repentance/willingness to go forward, forgiveness/the letting go of those things which impede your goals, and reconciliation/the quality of the renewal. (+++)

Now list the things/relationships that tend to limit or destroy your excitement and energy. (+++) Reflect on the degree of grace/unconditional acceptance that is present on your part. (+++) Using the Psychosynthesis definition of will, what is the degree of willing that is there to let go of that which is blocking this movement? (+++) How committed are you to be involved in the process of reconciliation/renewal? (+++)

We cannot be all things to all people. Determine how you will give your energies to those things and the relationships which have the greatest priority. Be willing to let go of things/relationships that are not a high priority. Make a list of things/relationship in order of importance/priority. (+++)

Pretend you have just been chosen as Man or Woman of the Year in your community. Write the newspaper article about yourself and why you were selected. (+++) As you write this article, please be sure to include those immortal qualities that will live beyond your physical self, as well as those notable things that are identified with your mortality. (+++)

A Concluding Word

The macrocosm or the large conflicts of the world cannot be resolved without the resolutions to the microcosm or inner struggles that we face. In effect, this is the premise of our writings.

We stated, earlier, that all matter is energy. One of the most fundamental aspects of our core-value belief system is that God is love, God is light, and God is energy. We cannot survive without love/light/energy—God. At the very heart of growth is the need to harmonize with the natural energies within and around us and live with the wisdom that is inherent in those energies.

In terms of our bodily functions, cellular action is at the very core of our becoming. If action at this level becomes dysfunctional, serious consequences within our body will soon be apparent.

In the same manner, we are part of the cellular structure of the larger society. This would imply that we must begin with ourselves if we are to change the world!

Jesus said that we are to be "the salt of the earth," or its agents of change. For change to occur, there must be risking. He also said that if we sought to save ourselves, we would lose the very thing we were trying to save. On the other hand, if we are willing to risk everything, then something of eternal significance will occur, something of the immortal can transpire.

At the heart of risking are grace, confession, repentance, forgiveness and reconciliation. Without these processes there can be little growth, little healing. This is the 'journey' to wholeness! While engagement in these processes can, indeed, be risky, to do otherwise is to choose a path of stagnation and death. The ancient prophets and priests challenged their people to choose between life or death. Their challenge is still relevant today.

Postscript from Eugene

Throughout the book, I have made a number of references to my relationship to my wife, Leta. She died on November 30, 2010. We were married three weeks short of sixty-two years. While our marriage was, at times less than idyllic, we had an incredible journey together. At her memorial service, I expressed my appreciation for her unfailing love and support as I made a number of truly daunting decisions that impacted our live together.

She faced her years with dementia, a condition that I have described as the emotional equivalent of leprosy where different aspects of the core personality simply fall away one dimension at a time, with great courage and dignity. While she often wept when we were alone when she spoke about her increasingly disability, she often displayed a sense of humor about her condition when she was in public. She often referred to me, for example, as her "memory bank" when she spoke of her failing memory.

Our daughter, in a moving tribute to her mother, noted that she had little preparation for living in a third world under third world conditions where we didn't, for example, have the luxury of a refrigerator in our home. Linda noted that her mother would ride a bicycle downtown to the open air market place where she would negotiate for food produce where a trade language which she didn't understand was used. She provided a secure and loving environment for her two elementary children, who attended local Dutch speaking schools, with superb competence.

Linda added that she was never aware of how high her mother's anxiety level must have experienced during the times that her husband would be gone for weeks on end piloting his plane over uncharted rain forest jungles with no prepared airstrips landing other than between rare spaces where there were no trees in the midst of the rain forest. During this time he was organizing and participating in expeditions that eventually contacted isolated Indians who had no previous contacts with the "outside world." Linda makes this telling comment about her mother.

"She handled these responsibilities in extremely difficult circumstances with much grace and dignity."

During the final year of her life, we together visited close friends in Thailand and Mexico, visited a former Rotary Exchange daughter now living in Peru, plus all of her living siblings and our off springs. She died in Wichita, Kansas when we were completing the final round of visits to our children.

I have been deeply enriched because we choose to make this fascinating journey of life together.

BIBLIOGRAPHY

Assagioli, Roberto, *Psychosynthesis*, Penguin Books, 1976

Canfield, Jack & Hanson, Mark, *Chicken Soup for the Soul,* Health Communications, Inc., 1993

Covey, Stephen, *7 Habits of Highly Effective People*, Simon and Schuster, 1989

Ferrucci, Piero, *What We May Be: Techniques for Psychological and Spiritual Growth,* J. D. Tarcher, Inc., 1982

Fox Matthew, *Original Blessing,* Bear Publishing, 1983.

Fromm Eric, *To Have or To Be,* Harper & Row, Publishers, San Francisco, 1976

Jones, Alan, *Passion for Pilgrimage,* Harper & Row, Publishers, San Francisco, 1989

Jourard, Sidney, *Transparent Self,* Van Nostrand, Princeton, 1964

Keck, L. Robert, *Sacred Eyes,* Knowledge Systems, Inc., 1992

Keck, L. Robert, *Sacred Quest: The Evolution and Future of the Human Soul,* Chrysalis Books, West Chester, Pennsylvania , 2000

Kohlberg, Lawrence, *Assessing Moral Development,* Harvard University, July, 1978

Lomax, Eric, *Railroad Man,* Jonathan Cape, London, 1995

MacLeish, Archibald, *The Eleanor Roosevelt Story,* Houghton & Mifflin, Boston, 1965

May, Rollo, *The Courage to Create,* W. W. Norton & Company, Inc., New York, 1975

Shehaded, Raja, *Samed: Journal of a West Bank Palestinian*, Adams, 1984

Shostrom, Everett, *Actualizing Therapy,* IdITS Publishers, 1976

Tournier, Paul, *Guilt and Grace: A Psychological Study,* Harper & Row, 1962

Tournier, Paul, *Strong and the Weak,* Westminister Press, Philadelphia, 1963

Vargiu, James, *Synthesis I: The Psychosynthesis Workbook,* Synthesis Press, 830 Woodside Road, Redwood, City, CA , 1977

White, E. B., *Charlotte's Web,* Harper-Collins, 1952

Yancey, Philip, *What's So Amazing About Grace,* Zondervan, 1997

SOURCE NOTES

In Chapter One: OVERVIEW

(1) Vargiu, James, *Synthesis l: The Psychosynthesis Workbook*, p. 60
(2) Ferrucci, Piero, *What We May Be: Techniques for Psychological and Spiritual Growth,* p. 43
(3) Assagioli, Roberto, *Psychosynthesis,* p. 17
(4) Ferrucci, Op. cit., p. 45
(5) Ferrucci, Ibid, p. 44
(6) Ferrucci, Ibid, p. 47
(7) Ferrucci, Ibid, p. 48
(8) Ferrucci, Ibid, p. 54
(9) Ferrucci, Ibid, p. 55
(10) Ferrucci, Ibid, p. 61
(11) Ferrucci, Ibid, p. 77-79
(12) Shostrom, Everett, *Actualizing Therapy*, p. 124
(13) Shostrom, Ibid, p. 4
(14) Tournier, Paul, *Guilt and Grace: A Psychological Study,* p.64

In Chapter Two: NATURE OF GRACE

(15) Yancey, Philip, What's So Amazing About Grace? p. 282

In Chapter Three: CONFESSION

(16) Jourard, Sidney, *Transparent Self,* p. 20
(17) Fromm, Eric, *To Have or To Be*, pp. 77-78

In Chapter Four: REPENTANCE

(18) May, Rollo, *Courage to Create*, pp. 41-42
(19) Keck, L. Robert, *Sacred Eyes*, p. 33

(20) Jones, Alan, *Passion for Pilgrimage*, p. 6
(21) Tournier, Paul, *Strong and Weak*
(23) Yancey, Op. cit., p 138

In Chapter Five: FORGIVENESS

(24) Fox, Matthew, *Original Blessing*, p.163
(25) Kohlberg, Lawrence, *Assessing Moral Development,* pp. 22-28

In Chapter Six: RECONCILIATION

(26) Shehadeh, Raja, *Samed: Journal of a West Bank Palestinian,* pp. 35-38
(27) *The Gospel Matthew*, chapter 5:43-48

In Chapter Seven: FACING THE FUTURE

(28) Canfield, Jack, & Hansen, Mark, *Chicken Soup for the Soul: 101 Stories to Open the Soul and Rekindle the Spirit,* p. 69
(29) MacLeish, Archibald, *The Eleanor Roosevelt Story,* Preface.
(30) Keck, Op. cit., p. 126
(31) Keck, Ibid, p. 139
(32) Keck, Ibid, p. 155
(33) Keck, Ibid, p. 160
(34) Keck, L. Robert, *Sacred Quest: The Evolution and Future of the Human Soul,* pp. 163f.
(35) Lomax, *Railroad Man*, pp. 263-267

AUTHORS

EUGENE FRIESEN, who attended a one-room school in western Nebraska, received a ThB from the Owosso Bible College in Owosso, Michigan in 1950 and a BA from Taylor University in 1951. After serving a small congregation in South Carolina as pastor, he received a military commission as an Army Chaplain and served five years of active duty, including a two-year stint with the 82nd Airborne Division.

Prior to returning to graduate school, he was a missionary bush pilot in Surinam, South America where he was the organizer of, and participant in, an expedition that contacted the Trio Indians who had not previously had contact with the outside world.

After completing his Ph.D. at Michigan State University, he was both the administrative as well as clinical director of a 100 bed psychiatric ward at the VA Hospital in Battle Creek, Michigan. He then became Director of a Mental Health Center in Lansing, Michigan.

Moving to Arizona, Dr. Friesen was a psychologist in private practice for nearly twenty years. With the coming of the health maintenance organizations, he made the decision to complete his professional life as a United Methodist pastor. Along with seventeen Roman Catholic priests, four sisters and two other Protestants, he participated in an exciting process that led to a D.Min. from the Jesuit School of Theology, Berkeley.

He retired in 2000 and has served as a lecturer on cruise ships. He has been a member of the Sons of Orpheus male choir since 1993 and makes regular trips to Thailand on Rotary-sponsored trips.

CARROLL A. RINEHART has served the education profession for more than sixty years. He has been a music teacher, music administrator, college instructor, school principal and an author and composer. He is co-author of *Music! Words! Opera!* (MMB Music, Inc. and OPERA America, Inc.), co-author of *Spectrum of Music!* (Macmillan Publishing Company) and collections of original songs for school-age students. He has composed two operas for church production: *How Was I to Know?* (a Christmas opera published by MMB Music, Inc. St. Louis) and an opera for Easter, *In the Shadow of the Cross* (performed but not published).

Dr. Rinehart received a BS in Music Education from Ashland University, and MA from Ohio State University and an honorary LHD from Ashland University. He has done additional graduate work at USC and the University of Arizona. He has conducted workshops throughout the United States and Canada and in Australia, Mexico and Hong Kong. As a consultant in opera education he has facilitated nearly 1,700 operas which school-age students have created and produced.

He continues to conduct research to determine how classes of students can achieve up to two years growth in less than a year as measured by standardized tests. This study is being conducted as an outgrowth of work with the MIENC (Music in Education National Consortium) and the New England Conservatory.

He is, also, a board member of the Society of Southwestern Authors and former president of the Arizona Music Educators Association, the Western Division Music Educators National Conference, the Arizona Arts Education and the Tucson Commission on Arts and Culture.

CPSIA information can be obtained at www.ICGtesting.com
Printed in the USA
BVOW030604280212

283946BV00004B/5/P